Jìn bù 1
进步

Reviewed by: Peking University,
School of Chinese as a Second Language

Written by: Xiaoming Zhu and Yu Bin
Series Editor: Katharine Carruthers

www.heinemann.co.uk
✓ Free online support
✓ Useful weblinks
✓ 24 hour online ordering

0845 630 33 33

iNet
International Networking for Educational Transformation

Specialist Schools and Academies Trust
THE SCHOOLS NETWORK

Heinemann
Part of Pearson

Heinemann is an imprint of Pearson Education Limited, a company incorporated in England and Wales, having its registered office at Edinburgh Gate, Harlow, Essex, CM20 2JE. Registered company number: 872828

www.pearsonschoolsandfecolleges.co.uk

Heinemann is a registered trademark of Pearson Education Limited

Text © Pearson Education Limited 2010

First published 2010

22
16

British Library Cataloguing in Publication Data
A catalogue record for this book is available from the British Library

ISBN 978 0 435 04113 7

Copyright notice
All rights reserved. No part of this publication may be reproduced in any form or by any means (including photocopying or storing it in any medium by electronic means and whether or not transiently or incidentally to some other use of this publication) without the written permission of the copyright owner, except in accordance with the provisions of the Copyright, Designs and Patents Act 1988 or under the terms of a licence issued by the Copyright Licensing Agency, Saffron House, 6–10 Kirby Street, London EC1N 8TS (www.cla.co.uk). Applications for the copyright owner's written permission should be addressed to the publisher.

Edited by Lauren Bourque
Typeset by Doug Hewitt and Krystyna Hewitt
Produced by g-and-w PUBLISHING
Original illustrations © Clive Goodyer, Doug Hewitt, Jade, Shiny Leung, Julie Pla, Pearson Education Ltd 2010
Illustrated by Clive Goodyer, Doug Hewitt, Jade, Shiny Leung, Julie Pla
Cover design by Siu Hang Wong
Picture research by Ingrid Booz Morejohn
Cover photo/illustration © Shutterstock/Eric Isselée/isaxar/backgarden/ Yan Vugenfirer /mandygodbehear
Printed in Great Britain by Ashford Colour Press Ltd.

Acknowledgements
We would like to thank Naomi Li, Linying Liu and Michelle Tate for their invaluable help in the development of this course. Thank you to Charonne Prosser for all her inspiration and patience and thanks to all at SSAT and Pearson who were involved in the project. Thanks to Jan Bell too.
We would like to thank the following SSAT Confucius Classrooms which are supported by the Chinese Language Council International, Hanban: Hummersknott School and Language College, Kingsford Community School and Language College, Katharine Lady Berkeley's School, Calday Grange Grammar School and Djanogly City Academy.
We would also like to thank Rowan Laxton of Alchemy Studios and all those involved with the recording: Shuang Zou, Tony Chen, Zhong Zheng, Lisa Lin, Qiao-Chu Ding, Lufu Si and Carole Boyd.

The author and publisher would like to thank the following individuals and organisations for permission to reproduce photographs:
(Key: b-bottom; c-centre; l-left; r-right; t-top)
Alamy Images: Blue Jean Images 44b, Dennis Drenner / Aurora Photos 45t, Glow Asia RF 59, 82, © GoGo Images Corporation 48, GoGo Images Corporation 43, Iain Masterton 27tl, M. Scott Brauer 60, © Pictorial Press Ltd 9tc, Victor Paul Borg 82(restaurant); **Corbis:** Kimimasa Mayama / Reuters 9br, KIN CHEUNG / Reuters 9tl; **DK Images:** Ian O'Leary 80br; **Getty Images:** Tungstar 9tr, Alex Livesey / Getty Images 41(Rebecca Adlinton), Alex Mares-Manton / Asia Images / Getty Images 66b, Antonio Mo / Iconica / Getty Images 45b, China Photos 44 cl, Goodshoot / Jupiter Images / Getty Images 27br, Jason Hosking / Stone / Getty Images 66t, JEFF HAYNES / AFP / Getty Images 41(Michael Jordan), Liu Jin, AFP 44tr, Massimo Cebrelli / Getty Images 41(Beckham), Phillip Jarrell 26, Rick Stewart/Allsport/Getty Images 9r, Sean Justice 85(boy, 3rd row), Toru Yamanaka / AFP / Getty Images 41(Zhang Yining), William West / AFP / Getty Images 41(Vanessa Williams); **Ingrid Booz Morejohn:** 27tr, 27bl, 58, 62, 67, 80tl, 81(Expensive restaurant), 84; **Lonely Planet Images:** Greg Elms / Lonely Planet Images 80bl, 81t; Pearson Education Ltd: Gareth Boden 46; **Reuters:** Claro Cortes 63; **Shutterstock:** Amy Nichole Harris 11b, Andrea Skjold 74l, Anna Nemkovich 81(Food stall), Claudio Zaccherini 10b, Flashon Studio 74r, Jarno Gonzalez Zarraonandia 11t, Kheng Guan Toh 81b, Lijuan Guo 10t, yung photographer@gmail.com / Shutterstock 80tr

All other images © Pearson Education

Every effort has been made to trace the copyright holders and we apologise in advance for any unintentional omissions. We would be pleased to insert the appropriate acknowledgement in any subsequent edition of this publication.

目录 Contents

1 嗨 hāi Hi!

1 一二三 yī èr sān	One, two, three, ...	Counting up to 99 and learning simple characters	2
2 你多大? nǐ duō dà	How old are you?	Talking about your age	4
3 你好 nǐ hǎo	Hello	Learning some basic greetings	6
4 我叫... wǒ jiào...	My name is ...	Introducing yourself and others	8
5 中国 zhōng guó	China	Discovering China	10
汉字 hàn zì	Investigating characters	Learning more about Chinese characters	12
Extension			14
Review			16
Test			17
Key language			18
Stroke order			19

2 家 jiā Family and home

1 我的家人 wǒ de jiā rén	My family	Talking about family using measure words	20
2 我的小猫 wǒ de xiǎo māo	My little cat	Talking about your pets	22
3 我的生日 wǒ de shēng rì	My birthday	Learning to say dates and months	24
4 中国人的家 zhōng guó rén de jiā	Chinese homes	Finding out about Chinese homes and families	26
汉字 hàn zì	Investigating characters	Learning more about Chinese characters	28
Extension			30
Review			32
Test			33
Key language			34
Stroke order			35

3 爱好 ài hào Hobbies

1 我们玩儿游戏吧! wǒ men wánr yóu xì ba	Let's play games!	Talking about what you do in your free time	36
2 我喜欢看电视! wǒ xǐ huan kàn diàn shì	I like watching TV!	Talking about what you like doing	38
3 你会游泳吗? nǐ huì yóu yǒng ma	Can you swim?	Talking about sport	40
4 我星期一上网 wǒ xīng qī yī shàng wǎng	I surf the net on Mondays.	Learning the days of the week	42
5 年轻人的爱好 nián qīng rén de ài hào	Young people's hobbies	Learning about young people's hobbies in China	44
汉字 hàn zì	Investigating characters	Learning more about Chinese characters	46
Extension			48
Review			50
Test			51
Key language			52
Stroke order			53

4 学校 xué xiào School

1 中文很酷! zhōng wén hěn kù	Chinese is cool!	Talking about school subjects	54
2 你几点上课? nǐ jǐ diǎn shàng kè	What time's your class?	Telling the time	56
3 我的课程表 wǒ de kè chéng biǎo	My timetable	Talking about your school timetable	58
4 你们班大不大? nǐ men bān dà bu dà	Is your class big?	Talking about school in China	60
5 中国的学校 zhōng guó de xué xiào	Schools in China	Discovering schools in China	62
汉字 hàn zì	Investigating characters	Learning more about Chinese characters	64
Extension			66
Review			68
Test			69
Key language			70
Stroke order			71

5 食品和饮料 shí pǐn hé yǐn liào Food and drink

1 我吃米饭 wǒ chī mǐ fàn	I eat rice	Talking about what you like to eat and drink	72
2 你午饭吃什么? nǐ wǔ fàn chī shén me	What do you have for lunch?	Talking about different kinds of food and drink	74
3 一日三餐 yí rì sān cān	Daily meals	Talking about mealtimes	76
4 我想喝可乐 wǒ xiǎng hē kě lè	I would like a coke.	Ordering in a restaurant	78
5 中国菜 zhōng guó cài	Chinese food	Regional food	80
汉字 hàn zì	Investigating characters	Learning more about Chinese characters	82
Extension			84
Review			86
Test			87
Key language			88
Stroke order			89

读和写 dú hé xiě Reading and Writing — 90

语法 Grammar — 100

写汉字 Writing Chinese characters — 113

辞典 Glossary – English/Chinese — 118

Introduction

Welcome to 进步 (Jìn bù)!

This is the first of two books designed to help you get started with Mandarin Chinese at Key Stage 3. We hope you'll enjoy the books as well as learning a lot from them.

This book has five chapters covering different topics. Each chapter is divided into different sections:

Core units

These include activities in all four skills – listening, reading, speaking and writing – to get you using Chinese straightaway. You'll find help with grammar and pronunciation as well.

Culture

Each chapter has one unit which gives you information about China and about how young people live. You'll have the chance to do research activities to find out more about everyday life.

Investigating characters

These pages will help you understand more about Chinese characters: how they developed over time and how they are constructed.

Key language

At the end of each chapter, you'll find a list of the key language you've been studying in that chapter, as well as grids showing you how the Chinese characters are written.

Grammar and Glossary

At the back of the book there is a grammar section where you can find explanations of all the grammar you'll be covering in the book, as well as some activities to practise it. There is also an English-Chinese wordlist for reference.

Good luck!

祝你学习进步!

1 嗨 hāi Hi!

① 一二三 yī èr sān One, two, three, …

Counting up to 99 and learning simple characters

LISTENING 1 Listen and repeat the numbers from 1–10.

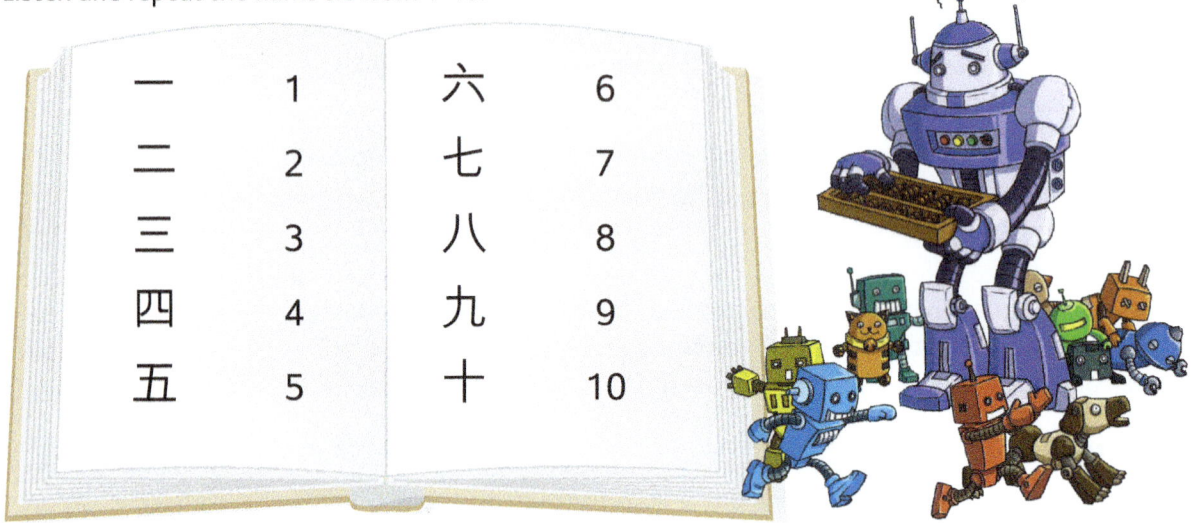

一	1	六	6
二	2	七	7
三	3	八	8
四	4	九	9
五	5	十	10

Language

Chinese characters

As you can see, Chinese looks very different to English or other languages you may already be studying. Chinese is written in characters rather than letters.
- One character may be one word, such as 六 which means 'six'.
- Characters might be put together in a sequence of two or three to make a word, such as 电脑 which means 'computer'.
- Characters in a sentence are always spaced equally, not grouped in words, such as 我是中国人。 This means 'I am Chinese'. You can see that full stops are a bit different too.

SPEAKING 2 In pairs, one person says a number in Chinese, the other says the English. Then swap roles.

A: 三　　　　B: three

READING 3 Note down the English for the following numbers.

| a 四 | b 二 | c 五 | d 一 |
| e 八 | f 九 | g 十 | h 六 |

LISTENING 4 Listen and write down the letter that matches the number you hear. (1–8)

Example: **1c**

| a 八 | b 五 | c 三 | d 四 |
| e 七 | f 一 | g 十 | h 二 |

2 二

Chapter 1 嗨

Language

Strokes and stroke order

Strokes are a series of lines that make up a character. There are a limited number of strokes. Each type of stroke is always written in the same direction, such as from left to right for a horizontal stroke.

The first two strokes you'll learn are:

Stroke	Rule to write the stroke	Example character
一	From left to right	二 (the top stroke is written first)
丨	From top to bottom	十 (the horizontal is written first)

WRITING 5 Practise writing the characters using what you have learned about strokes and stroke order.

一　二　三　十

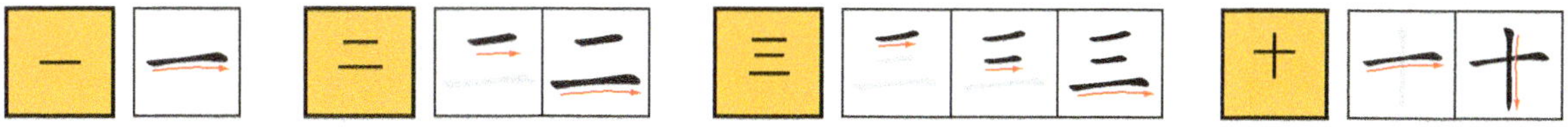

LISTENING 6 Listen and repeat the numbers from 11–20.

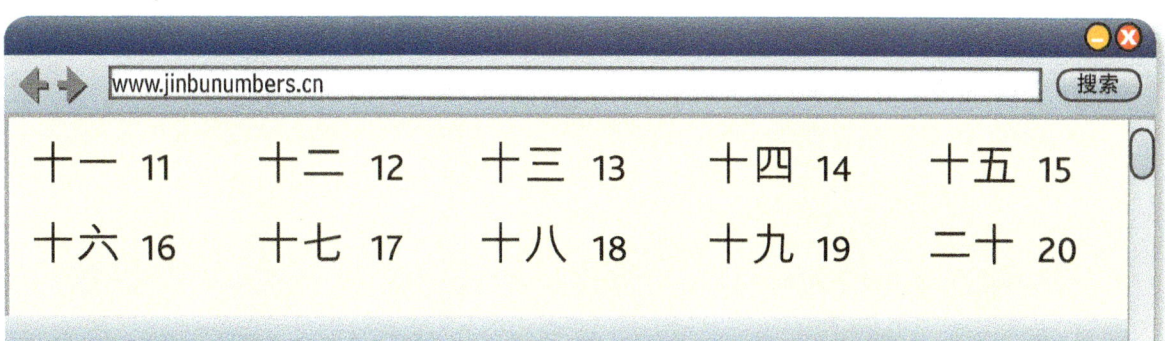

www.jinbunumbers.cn 　搜索

十一 11　十二 12　十三 13　十四 14　十五 15
十六 16　十七 17　十八 18　十九 19　二十 20

READING 7 Complete the sequences. Find the correct number for each gap from the list. You can use the same numbers more than once.

Example: **1 c**

a 十　b 四　c 一　d 三　e 五　f 十四
g 十三　h 十八　i 六　j 八　k 七　l 十六

_1_ 二 _2_ 四
三 _3_ _4_ _5_ 七
二 四 _6_ _7_ 十
一 三 _8_ _9_ 九
_10_ 十一 十二 _11_ 12 十五
十二 十四 _13_ _14_ 二十

Grammar

Numbers

Learning numbers in Chinese is really easy! Numbers above 10 are simple to remember, you just say '10 1', '10 2', etc. for 十一 (11), 十二 (12). For higher numbers, you say '2 10', '3 10', etc. – that is, 二十 (20), 三十 (30), so '4 10 2' 四十二 would be 42.

三 3

2 你多大？ nǐ duō dà How old are you?

🌸 Talking about your age

LISTENING 1 Listen and note down the letter of the correct picture. (1–6)

Example: **1 a**

a b  c 
d  e  f

READING 2 Copy and complete the grid with the correct age.

1 Jake   十二岁
2 Louisa   十一岁
3 Shabaz   八岁
4 Elly   十六岁
5 Lily   七岁
6 Jason   九岁

Name	Age
Jake	12

Grammar

Talking about age

In English, when you talk about someone's age, you say: *person + verb to be* (am/is/are) + *age*, such as 'I am 11 years old'. In Chinese there is no need for a verb; you just need to say: *person + age +* 岁 suì, for example 我八岁。 wǒ bā suì 'I am eight years old'.

LISTENING 3 Listen to the conversations. Note down the ages in English. (1–5)

你多大？ nǐ duō dà   How old are you?
我 … 岁。 wǒ … suì   I am … years old.

Grammar

Asking about age

To ask someone's age, you just use the question word and the pronoun or name (you, he, she, Jade, etc.). So in English, we say 'How old are you?' This becomes 你多大？ nǐ duō dà, literally 'You how big?', in Chinese.

4 四

Chapter 1 嗨

READING 4 Read the conversations and match them to the correct picture.

我 wǒ I
你 nǐ you

1 你多大？我六岁。
2 你多大？我十七岁。
3 你多大？我二十岁。
4 你多大？我五岁。
5 你多大？我十四岁。

SPEAKING 5 In pairs, ask and answer about ages.

A: 你多大？
B: 我 ... 岁。

1　10 years old
2　9 years old
3　13 years old
4　15 years old
5　12 years old

Language

Tones

To pronounce Chinese properly, you need to understand tones. Lots of characters have the same sound in Chinese; using the correct tones will help make sure that the person listening to you knows what you are talking about. There are four main tones in Mandarin Chinese:

- 1st tone: High and flat, for example sān 三
- 2nd tone: Going up, for example shí 十
- 3rd tone: Down and up, for example wǔ 五
- 4th tone: Going down, for example liù 六

LISTENING 6 First listen and repeat the sounds which have different tones. Then listen and note down the tone for each sound. (1–4)

SPEAKING 7 Copy and complete the grid with the correct sounds, marking the tones over the vowel on each one and then practise pronouncing them.

1　yi　　4　da
2　ni　　5　san
3　ba

	1st tone	2nd tone	3rd tone	4th tone
1 yi	yī	yí	yǐ	yì
2				

五 5

③ 你好 nǐ hǎo Hello

Learning some basic greetings

LISTENING 1 Look at the pictures. Listen and repeat the greetings. (1–6)

1. 你好！
2. 再见！
3. 早上好！
4. 老师好！ 你好！
5. 忙不忙？ 很忙。
6. 老师再见！ 再见！

你好	nǐ hǎo	hello (to one person)	
早上好	zǎo shang hǎo	good morning	
再见	zài jiàn	good-bye	
老师好	lǎo shī hǎo	hello teacher	
忙不忙？	máng bu máng	are you busy?	
很忙	hěn máng	very busy	

Culture

Greetings

忙不忙？ máng bu máng is a common phrase used to greet people. It is a question literally meaning 'Busy or not busy?' You could reply 很忙 hěn máng, 'very busy' or 不忙 bù máng, 'not busy'.

SPEAKING 2 In pairs, practise the greetings from Activity 1.

A: 早上好！
B: 你好！

6 六

Chapter 1 嗨

3 Listen to the conversations and choose the letter of the correct picture for each one. (1–4)

Example: **1 a**

4 Match the greetings and the responses.

1 早上好!
2 你好!
3 忙不忙？
4 老师再见!

a 再见!
b 不忙。
c 你好!
d 早上好!

Pinyin

It can be difficult to remember how to say Chinese characters so learners usually use pinyin to help them. Pinyin is a form of writing Chinese sounds in roman letters with the tone markers.
- In this book, it usually appears alongside a character, such as 六 liù.
- Apart from when they first start school, native speakers of Chinese don't use pinyin, so it's important to try to remember how to say the characters and not rely on pinyin.

5 In pairs, one person says a greeting phrase in Chinese and the other gives the correct English, then swap roles. Use Activity 1 to help you.

6 Put the phrases in the order you hear them. (1–6)

Example: **1 d**

a Good-bye.
b Good morning.
c Hello teacher.
d Hello.
e Are you busy?
f Very busy.

7 Practise writing the following key character for this unit. Remember: left to right and top to bottom.

早

七 7

4 我叫 ... wǒ jiào ... My name is ...

🌸 Introducing yourself and others

LISTENING 1 Who is speaking? Put the pictures in the order you hear them. (1–5)

1. zhōu jìng
我叫周静。

2. dèng wēi
我叫邓薇。

3. wáng xiǎo jǐn
我叫王小瑾。

4. guō fēi fei
我叫郭飞飞。

5. lǐ léi
我叫李雷。

Grammar

Verbs

Verbs in Chinese are simple! Unlike other foreign languages you may have studied, in Chinese the form of the verb stays the same whatever the subject (he, she, you, etc.).

My name is Tom. (I *am* called Tom.) 我叫 Tom。
Your name is Grace. (You *are* called Grace.) 你叫 Grace。

In both sentences the verb 叫 jiào stays the same.

SPEAKING 2 In pairs, practise asking each other's name.

A: 你叫什么?
B: 我叫...

你叫什么? nǐ jiào shén me
What is your name?

Grammar

Asking someone's name

When asking about names, the question word goes at the end of the sentence: 'What is your name?' 你叫什么? nǐ jiào shén me literally 'You are called what?'

8 八

Chapter 1 嗨

LISTENING 3 Listen to Lin Fang telling you about some famous Chinese people. You could use the Internet to find out more about them. (1–5)

1 杨澜 yáng lán, 42
2 成龙 chéng lóng, 56 
3 李宁 lǐ níng, 46 
4 刘翔 liú xiáng, 26 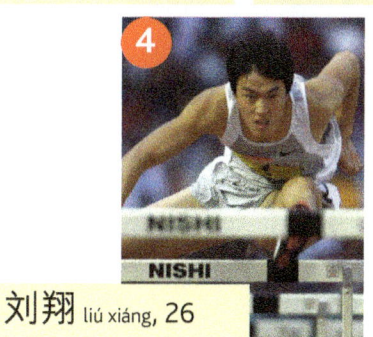
5 邓亚萍 dèng yà píng, 37 

Language

He/She

In Chinese the words for 'he' and 'she' have different characters:

he 他
she 她

but they are pronounced the same: tā
The context will usually make it clear which one is being used.

READING 4 Copy and complete the grid.

Name	Age
1 dà míng	

1 你好！我叫大明 dà míng，我十二岁。

2 你好！我叫丽丽 lì lì，我十五岁。你多大？

3 你好！我叫张一天 zhāng yī tiān，我十三岁。你叫什么？你多大？

LISTENING 5 Listen and choose the correct answer (1–4).

Example: 1 b

1　a You are　b I am　c She is　　　called Lanlan.
2　a You are　b I am　c She is　　　called Carol.
3　a You are　b I am　c He is　　　called Naveed.
4　a I am　　b She is　c The teacher is　called Li Dawen.

SPEAKING 6 Use the pictures in Activity 3 and take it in turns to ask and answer questions about them. Use the sample dialogue on the right to help you.

A: 她叫什么？
B: 她叫杨澜。
A: 她多大？
B: 她四十二岁。

WRITING 7 Practise writing the following key character for this unit. Remember: left to right and top to bottom.

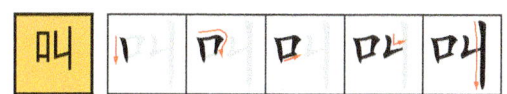

叫　丨　冂　口　叫　叫

九 9

⑤ 中国 zhōng guó China

🌸 Discovering China

About China

Population: 1.3 billion
Size: 9.6 million square km
Ethnic groups: 56
Famous landmark: The Great Wall
Famous rivers: Yangtze River and Yellow River

北京 Beijing

Beijing is the capital of China with a population of 17 million people; its name literally means 'north capital'. It is a thriving, modern city, but you can still see some of the alleyways and single-storey courtyard houses which were the main feature of the city right up until the 1980s. There is a lot of traffic, but many cyclists too. It is very cold in the winter and you can skate on the lakes in parks all over Beijing; in the summer, these lakes all have rowing boats for Beijingers to hire. Beijing held the 2008 Olympic Games. Tourists from all over the world visit Beijing to see the Great Wall of China, the Forbidden City, the Temple of Heaven and maybe even to fly a kite on Tiananmen Square. Mandarin Chinese, which you are learning, is based on the Beijing dialect.

上海 Shanghai

Located on China's eastern coast at the mouth of the Yangtze River, Shanghai is the largest city in China with over 20 million people; its name literally means 'on sea'. It is a large centre of commerce and finance. The city is known for its historical landmarks such as the Bund (the buildings on the waterfront are similar to the waterfront of one of its sister cities, Liverpool) and the Yuyuan Garden. Shanghai is also known for its modern skyline including the Oriental Pearl Tower, confirming its traditional name as the 'Pearl of the Orient' and its long-held reputation – at least in the eyes of its own residents - as the country's centre of culture and fashion. Shanghai residents speak Shanghainese but nearly all will be able to speak Mandarin too.

Chapter 1 嗨

西安 Xi'an

Xi'an literally means 'west peace', and is one of the oldest cities in China. The city served as the imperial capital of China during the reign of many Chinese emperors. The famous Silk Road started from here, a caravan route which played an important part in the exchange of trade and thought between China and the West. The First Emperor Qin Shi Huang had his underground army built here over 2,000 years ago, which is now the world famous Terracotta Army attracting visitors from all over the world to look at the warriors and marvel at how no two warriors are exactly alike. Xi'an is also full of other historical places of interest including the Big Wild Goose Pagoda, the Bell Tower and the City Wall.

香港 Hong Kong

Situated on China's south coast, with its name literally meaning 'fragrant harbour', Hong Kong is made up of a peninsula and 236 islands. Hong Kong is mountainous with a bustling and beautiful harbour; it is one of the world's top financial centres, but also a centre for shopping, food, music and cinema. No visit is complete without a ride on the Star Ferry and a visit to the Po Lin monastery to see Hong Kong's 34 metre high Buddha. People from all over the world live and work here, making it a truly international city. The locals in Hong Kong speak Cantonese, but also Mandarin.

READING 1 Match the numbers and the letters to make four correct place names. Then give the meanings in English of the characters in each place name.

1	西	a	海
2	香	b	安
3	北	c	港
4	上	d	京

READING 2 Read about these places in China. Then, in small groups, do some research on Kunming. Put together a short presentation. Use the following questions to help you decide what to include.

- What is the population?
- Which languages are spoken there?
- What kind of costumes do some of the ethnic groups traditionally wear?
- Which places do most visitors to Kunming and the area around it go to see?

You could use characters and pictures to illustrate your presentation.

汉字 hàn zì **Investigating characters**

Learning more about Chinese characters

Chinese characters were originally pictures of many things. But over the centuries, the written characters have changed a lot and the majority of them no longer look like the things they represent.

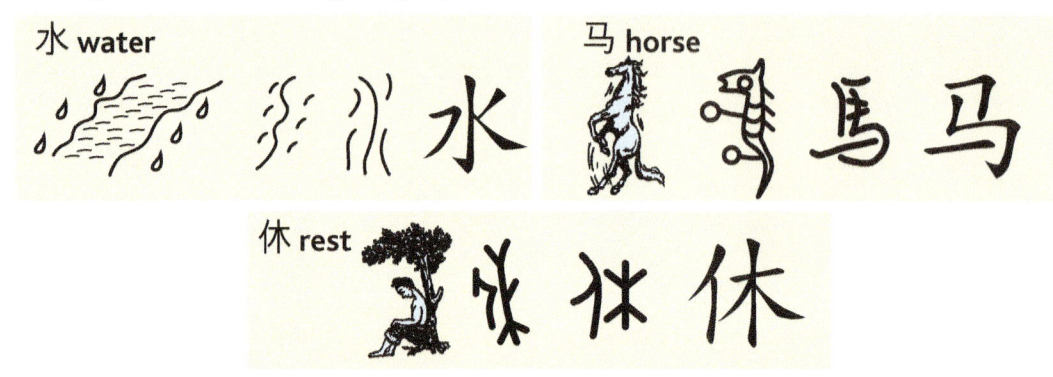

水 water

马 horse

休 rest

READING 1 Can you match the modern characters and their original pictures? Then say in English what they are.

1. 山
2. 鼠
3. 火
4. 雨
5. 伞
6. 飞

a. (rain cloud)
b. (umbrella)
c. (mouse)
d. (bird)
e. (fire)
f. (mountains)

WRITING 2 Practise writing the following characters. Remember: left to right and top to bottom.

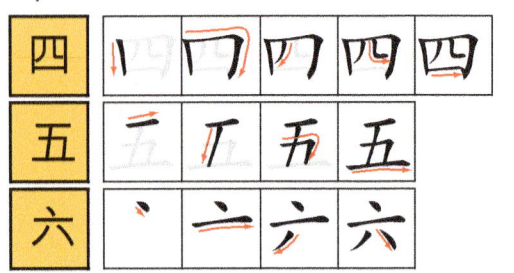

四 五 六 七 八 九

Stroke	English name	Example character
丶	The dot	六
丿	The sweeping left stroke	九 八
乀	The sweeping right stroke	八
乛	Turning stroke	四 五 早 叫

12 十二

Chapter 1 嗨

READING 3 Count the strokes of the following characters.

1. 七
2. 九
3. 你
4. 五
5. 四
6. 叫
7. 早
8. 不

部首 bù shǒu Radicals

Radicals are parts of Chinese characters which can give you clues about the meaning of the character.

For example, 女 is a Chinese character that means 'female'. It often appears as part of other characters. You've already seen the character 她 which means 'she'.

As you learn Chinese, you'll be introduced to radicals which can help you remember characters more easily and know something about the meanings of characters you haven't seen before.

口 is a radical meaning 'mouth'. Can you work out why the character 叫 has this radical?

READING 4 Can you find these radicals in the following characters? Then match the characters to their meaning with the help of the radicals.

Example: **a 4** – to talk

a	讠 = speech	1	鸭		meal
b	饣 = food	2	雪		tea
c	艹 = plant/grass	3	拳		fist
d	手 = hand	4	说		duck
e	父 = father	5	饭		snow
f	鸟 = bird	6	爸		dad
g	雨 = rain	7	茶		to talk

十三 13

Extension

LISTENING 1 Listen and say whether the statements are true or false. (1–8)

1. The conversation is between two friends.
2. The conversation is taking place in the morning.
3. This person is introducing himself.
4. This person is introducing herself.
5. This is a teenager introducing himself.
6. This is a teenager introducing herself.
7. This person is asking for someone's name.
8. This person is greeting someone.

SPEAKING 2 Introduce the following people with their name and age.

大伟 dà wěi
age 11

Maya
age 14

SPEAKING 3 Make up a dialogue asking and answering about name and age. Do it with at least three partners. You could make up your name and age for different partners.

A: 你叫什么？
B: 我叫 Anya。

A: 你多大？
B: 我十一岁。

WRITING 4 Count the strokes of the characters and note down the total. Then write the number of the strokes in Chinese.

Example: a 2 二

a 八　　b 九　　c 四　　d 五

e 岁　　f 叫　　g 早　　h 你

14 十四

Chapter 1 嗨

5 Read the sentences and choose the correct English translation.

Example: 1 b

1 我十岁。
    a I am 11 years old.   b I am 10 years old.

2 他十九岁。
    a He is 19 years old.   b He is 17 years old.

3 我叫 Robert。他叫 John。
    a He is called John and I am called Robert.   b I am called John and he is called Robert.

4 你十八岁,我十六岁。
    a You are 18 years old and I am 16.   b I am 18 years old and you are 16.

5 他五岁,他叫 Simon.
    a I am 5 years old and I am called Simon.   b He is 5 years old and he is called Simon.

6 她十二岁,他二十岁。
    a She is 12 years old and he is 20.   b She is 20 years old and he is 12.

6 Write the Chinese for the following numbers.

5   13   38   9   76   14   10   25

7 Complete the following phrases/sentences with the appropriate characters. Then write the phrases/sentences in English.

Example: 我<u>十四</u> (14) 岁。   I am 14 years old.

<u> 1 </u> 上好。

我 <u> 2 </u> Robert 。

他 <u> 3 </u> Scott, 他 <u> 4 </u> (12) 岁。

她 <u> 5 </u> Alice, 她三岁。

<u> 6 </u> 上好, 他 <u> 7 </u> Anthony, 他 <u> 8 </u> (26) 岁。

十五 15

Review

I can:

①
- count up to 99 — 一 yī, 二 èr, 三 sān, 四 sì, 五 wǔ
  二十 èr shí, 三十 sān shí, 四十 sì shí, 五十 wǔ shí...
- write numbers 1–3 — 一、二、三
- understand basic strokes — horizontal stroke, vertical stroke, etc.

②
- say how old I am — 我十一岁。 wǒ shí yī suì
- ask people's age — 你多大？ nǐ duō dà
- understand simple written sentences about age — 你多大？我十四岁。
- understand the four tones — yī yí yǐ yì

③
- say and respond to basic greetings — 你好 nǐ hǎo, 早上好 zǎo shang hǎo, 老师好 lǎo shī hǎo, 忙不忙 máng bu máng, 再见 zài jiàn
- recognise written greetings — 你好、早上好、老师好、忙不忙、再见
- understand pinyin — nǐ hǎo, zài jiàn

④
- say what my name is — 我叫 wǒ jiào...
- say what other people's names are — 他叫 tā jiào..., 她叫 tā jiào...
- ask people's names — 你叫什么? nǐ jiào shén me

Investigating characters
- Write the numbers up to 20 — 十四、十五、十六、十七、十八...
- Write the key characters for the chapter — 早、叫
- Recognise simple radicals — 女、口

16 十六

Chapter 1 嗨

Test

1 **LISTENING** Listen and say whether the information is true or false (1–4).
1 Lanlan   13 years old
2 Scott   9 years old
3 Mei Fang 14 years old
4 Mark   11 years old

2 **SPEAKING** Pretend you are the highlighted person in the group. Introduce yourself and other members in the group with their names and ages.

Example: **1** 我叫 Liz，我十三岁。他叫 Ming，他十五岁。她叫 Marie，她十四岁。

① Ming 15 Liz 13 Marie 14
② Philip 16 Kyle 13 Nila 17
③ John 11 Meilan 10 George 9
④ Joanna 9 Poppy 4 Ben 2

3 **READING** Match the Chinese to the English.

Example: **1c**

1 你好   2 早上好   3 他   4 她
5 十   6 十九   7 二十 8 十七

a 17   b he   c hello   d good morning   e she   f 19   g 10   h 20

4 **WRITING** Choose the correct characters and write them down to fill in the gaps.

___1___ 上好。   a 好   b 早

我十 ___2___ 岁。   a 五   b 十

他 ___3___ 三岁。   a 十   b 五

我 ___4___ Dominic。 a 早   b 叫

十七 17

Key language

Numbers and age

一	yī	one	十五	shí wǔ	fifteen
二	èr	two	十六	shí liù	sixteen
三	sān	three	十七	shí qī	seventeen
四	sì	four	十八	shí bā	eighteen
五	wǔ	five	十九	shí jiǔ	nineteen
六	liù	six	二十	èr shí	twenty
七	qī	seven	三十	sān shí	thirty
八	bā	eight	四十	sì shí	forty
九	jiǔ	nine	五十	wǔ shí	fifty
十	shí	ten	岁	suì	years old
十一	shí yī	eleven	你多大？	nǐ duō dà	How old are you?
十二	shí èr	twelve	你	nǐ	you
十三	shí sān	thirteen	我…岁	wǒ … suì	I am … years old.
十四	shí sì	fourteen	我	wǒ	I

Greetings

你好	nǐ hǎo	hello	忙不忙？	máng bu máng	(Are you) busy?
早上好	zǎo shang hǎo	good morning	很忙	hěn máng	very busy
老师好	lǎo shī hǎo	hello teacher	不忙	bù máng	not busy
再见	zài jiàn	good-bye			

Introductions

叫	jiào	to be called	你叫什么？	nǐ jiào shén me	What is your name?
他	tā	he	什么？	shén me	What?
她	tā	she	我叫…	wǒ jiào…	My name is…

Stroke order

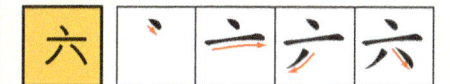

一	一
二	一 二
三	一 二 三
四	丨 冂 四 四 四
五	一 丅 五 五
六	丶 亠 六 六
七	一 七
八	丿 八
九	丿 九
十	一 十
早	丨 冂 曰 旦 早
叫	丨 冂 口 叫 叫

2 家 jiā Family and home

1 我的家人 wǒ de jiā rén My family

🌸 Talking about family using measure words

LISTENING 1 Listen and note down the names and ages of the family members. (1–6)

妈妈 mā ma   爸爸 bà ba   哥哥 gē ge   姐姐 jiě jie   我 wǒ   弟弟 dì di   妹妹 mèi mei

Example: 1 Julia 49

1 mum
2 dad
3 older brother
4 older sister
5 younger brother
6 younger sister

Grammar

The use of 和 hé

和 hé, which means 'and', is only used between nouns. It is not used to connect clauses or sentences in Chinese. Notice the difference:

爸爸和妈妈 = dad **and** mum

爸爸叫 Robert, 妈妈叫 Selina。 = Dad is called Robert, (and) mum is called Selina.

SPEAKING 2 In pairs, take it in turns to ask and answer questions about the people in Activity 1.

A: 妈妈叫什么? mā ma jiào shén me
B: 妈妈叫 Julia。 mā ma jiào Julia
A: 妈妈多大? mā ma duō dà
B: 妈妈四十九岁。 mā ma sì shí jiǔ suì

有 yǒu to have
没有 méi yǒu not to have

LISTENING 3 Listen to these people talking about their families. Choose the correct option. (1–4)

1 Daming has a younger **brother/sister**.
2 Fatima has a **younger/older** brother and a **younger/older** sister.
3 Dongdong is **13/14** years old and has an older **sister/brother**.
4 Xiaolan is **7/8** years old and has an **older/younger** sister.

Grammar

Measure words

Measure words are also used in English, for example, one **cup** of tea or three **pieces** of paper. In Chinese, you must always put a measure word between a number and a noun:

number + measure word + noun.

The most commonly used measure word is 个 ge:

一个姐姐 yí ge jiě jie
one older sister

三个弟弟 sān ge dì di
three younger brothers

20 二十

Chapter 2 家

READING 4 Read about Jamar's and Derry's families. Note down in English the details of each family.

1
你好！我叫 Derry，我十一岁，我有一个哥哥和两个姐姐，我没有弟弟和妹妹。

2
早上好！他叫 Jamar，他二十岁。他有一个姐姐和一个弟弟。

Language

The use of 二 èr and 两 liǎng

Both these words mean 'two'. Use 二 in counting or saying a number by itself, such as 二十. To talk about an amount of something, use 两:

两个妹妹 liǎng ge mèi mei = two younger sisters

家 jiā home/family

我家 wǒ jiā my home/family

口 kǒu measure word for total number of people in a family

人 rén person

LISTENING 5 Listen and answer the questions in English.

1 How many people are in the family?
2 Does this person have an older sister?
3 How old is the older brother?
4 Who is 14 years old?

Grammar

The use of 口 kǒu

口 kǒu is a measure word which is used to describe the total number of people in a family. 口 literally means 'mouth', so here it means the number of mouths to feed. For example:

他家有三口人。 tā jiā yǒu sān kǒu rén = His family has three people. (There are three people in his family.)

SPEAKING 6 Work in groups of three or four and take turns to introduce your family. You can make up the details if you want to.

- Give your name and age.
- Say how many people are in your family.
- Say how many brothers and sisters you have.
- Give their names and ages.
- Say what you don't have in your family.
- Don't forget to include measure words!

WRITING 7 Practise writing the following key characters for this unit. Remember: left to right and top to bottom. Look at page 35 for more help with stroke order.

| 有 | 个 | 口 | 人 |

二十一 21

② 我的小猫 wǒ de xiǎo māo — My little cat

Talking about your pets

LISTENING 1 Listen and note down the letter of the correct picture. (1–6)

a 鸟 niǎo b 狗 gǒu c 兔子 tù zi d 猫 māo e 鱼 yú f 蛇 shé

LISTENING 2 Listen and note down the pet and number in English next to the correct measure word in pinyin. (1–6)

Example: zhī: cat 1

tiáo:

Grammar

Measure words 只 zhī and 条 tiáo

Different measure words are used for different categories of things. The most common measure word used for animals and birds is 只, as in 一只鸟 yì zhī niǎo = one bird, 三只狗 sān zhī gǒu = three dogs. 条 is used for animals with a long thin body, for example 一条蛇 yì tiáo shé = one snake.

Try to learn the right measure word whenever you learn a new noun.

SPEAKING 3 In pairs, take it in turns to describe the pictures.

Example: A: 三只狗 B: 1

1 2 3 4 5 6

READING 4 Read the sentences, then copy and complete the grid with the details of who has which pets.

Who						
Kyle						

1 Kyle 有一只狗。
2 妈妈有三只兔子。
3 弟弟有一只狗，四条鱼。
4 老师有一只鸟。
5 哥哥有一条蛇，一只狗。
6 姐姐有狗吗？
   姐姐有两只猫，她没有狗。

Grammar

The use of 吗 ma

When you ask a yes/no question (questions that normally need a 'yes' or 'no' when you answer them in English), you just need to add 吗 ma at the end of the sentence to turn it into a yes/no question.

Statement	Yes/no question
你有狗。	你有狗吗？
她有弟弟。	她有弟弟吗？

22 二十二

Chapter 2 家

5 Listening
Listen to the conversations and choose the correct picture and label for each one. (1–5)

大 dà big
小 xiǎo small

Example: 1 g n

a b c d e
f g h i j

k 大兔子　l 小兔子　m 大猫　n 小猫　o 大鱼
p 小鱼　　q 大鸟　　r 小鸟　s 大狗　t 小狗

6 Speaking
In pairs, ask and answer questions pretending to have the pets below.

宠物 chǒng wù pet

A: 你有宠物吗？ nǐ yǒu chǒng wù ma
B: 我有一只大鸟。 wǒ yǒu yì zhī dà niǎo

1 one big bird
2 two small cats
3 one big dog
4 one snake
5 one small rabbit and five fish

Grammar
Adjectives (describing words)

For a simple adjective that is one syllable/character (such as 大 dà = big, 小 xiǎo = small), you just need to add it before the noun you're describing:

一只大猫 = one big cat
三只小狗 = three small dogs

Don't forget that you still need the correct measure word.

7 Writing
Practise writing the following key characters 大 and 小 for this unit.

大　小

8 Writing
Pretend you are Daniel or Bibi and complete the passage about your family. Use the text to help you.

我叫方林(fāng lín)，我十三岁。我家有四口人。我有爸爸、妈妈、一个姐姐。我有一只狗，姐姐有一只猫，爸爸妈妈有三条鱼。

我 __1__ Bibi/Daniel, 我家 __2__ 五 __3__ 人，爸爸、妈妈、一 __4__ 姐姐，__5__ 个哥哥 / 妹妹。我家 __6__ 一只猫，三 __7__ 鸟，__8__ 条鱼。

Daniel, 13 years old
Grace, 17 years old
Bibi, 9 years old

二十三 23

3 我的生日 wǒ de shēng rì My birthday

🌸 Learning to say dates and months

1 Match the English and Chinese.

日 rì date 月 yuè month

Example: **1 h**

1	January	5	May	9	September
2	February	6	June	10	October
3	March	7	July	11	November
4	April	8	August	12	December

a 三月	d 五月	g 八月	j 四月
b 十一月	e 六月	h 一月	k 七月
c 二月	f 九月	i 十二月	l 十月

Grammar

Months of the year

月 yuè is the Chinese word for 'month'. You just need to add the right number before 月 to make a month: for example, 一月 for January, 二月 for February, etc.

To say the date, use 日 after the number, for example, 二十三日 = 23rd. The month **always** goes before the day in Chinese, so 5 October would be 十月五日.

2 Listen and choose the correct answer. (1–6)

Example: **1a**

1	a 3 January	b 1 March	4	a 12 September	b 20 August
2	a 13 June	b 13 May	5	a 9 November	b 11 September
3	a 6 February	b 2 June	6	a 17 October	b 17 April

3 In pairs, say the following dates in Chinese.

5 January

8 February

11 July

16 October

25 December

Your birthday

Grammar

The use of 的 de

In Chinese, the possessive is made by adding 的 de after the pronoun (I, you, he, etc.) or noun.

我 I	我的 my (我的生日 my birthday)
你 you	你的 your
他 he	他的 his
她 she	她的 her
妈妈 mum	妈妈的 mum's (妈妈的生日 mum's birthday)

的 is often omitted where there is a close relationship, such as 我(的)家 = my family/home; 他(的)哥哥 = his older brother.

24 二十四

Chapter 2 家

READING 4 True or false? If false, write down the correct translation in English.

生日 shēng rì birthday
今天 jīn tiān today
是 shì to be

1 今天是十二月六日。 Today is 6 December.

2 我的生日是九月三日。 My birthday is 3 July.

3 我的生日是八月五日。 My birthday is 8 May.

4 我爸爸的生日是一月二日。 My mum's birthday is 1 February.

5 他的生日是十一月二十四日。 Her birthday is 24 November.

LISTENING 5 Listen, then copy and complete the grid with the correct age and birthday. (1–6)

Name	Age	Birthday
Chen Sheng	8	5 March
Josie		

WRITING 6 Practise writing the following key characters 日 月 生 是 for this unit. Remember: finish what is inside the box before you close it.

日 月 生 是

READING 7 Read the text and answer the questions in English.

我叫小月,我十三岁,我的生日是五月十一日。
我家有三口人,爸爸、妈妈和我。我爸爸
四十六岁,我妈妈四十三岁。我有一只猫。

1 What is this person's name? What does her name mean literally?
2 How old is she?
3 When is her birthday?
4 How many people are there in her family?
5 Who is 43 years old?
6 Does she have any pets?

WRITING 8 Complete the sentences according to the pictures.

我 __1__ Li Ming 。我 __2__ __3__ 岁。

我 __4__ Ding Jie,我 __5__ __6__ 岁,我有 __7__ __8__ 狗。

Li Ming
13 years old

Ding Jie
14 years old

二十五 25

4 中国人的家 zhōng guó rén de jiā — Chinese homes

Finding out about Chinese homes and families

Family structure

In Chinese families there are specific titles for each family member. For example, as you have already learned, there are different titles for older brother and younger brother, for older sister and younger sister. For the extended family, there are more complicated titles. It depends not only on whether the relative is older or younger than you, male or female, but also depends on whether they are from your mother's side or father's side. 'Cousin' in English can be expressed by 8 different words in Chinese! Below are some examples:

	Father's side	Mother's side
Grandmother	奶奶 (nǎi nai)	姥姥 (lǎo lao)
Grandfather	爷爷 (yé ye)	姥爷 (lǎo ye)

	Father's side (older than you)	Father's side (younger than you)	Mother's side (older than you)	Mother's side (younger than you)
Cousin (male)	堂哥 (táng gē)	堂弟 (táng dì)	表哥 (biǎo gē)	表弟 (biǎo dì)
Cousin (female)	堂姐 (táng jiě)	堂妹 (táng mèi)	表姐 (biǎo jiě)	表妹 (biǎo mèi)

When you address people in your family, particularly those who are older than you, you always use their family title. So, for example, when someone speaks to their older brother/sister, they would call them 哥哥 gē ge/姐姐 jiě jie instead of calling them by their name.

READING 1 Can you work out what you would call these people in Chinese?

1. Your mum's mum
2. Your dad's mum
3. Your male cousin (on your father's side and younger than you)
4. Your female cousin (on your mother's side and older than you)

Three generations living together

In China it is still common for three generations to live under the same roof, both in rural areas and cities. Grandparents look after their grandchildren while the parents go to work. There are not many part-time jobs available in China, so many working parents have to rely on the grandparents to take and collect their children to and from nursery/school, as well as to help with housework.

26 二十六

A flat or a sì hé yuàn courtyard?

Most people in Beijing, and many other Chinese cities, live in high-rise flats. However, some people still live in a sì hé yuàn courtyard; the name literally means 'a courtyard surrounded by four buildings' – one-storey houses traditionally lived in by people from the same extended family. The courtyards are built in areas known as hú tong (little alleys).

READING 2

In groups, do some research on sì hé yuàn courtyard/hú tong and have a discussion on the advantages/disadvantages of living in a sì hé yuàn. Try answering the following questions:

1 What does a typical sì hé yuàn look like?

2 What is a hú tong?

3 Many hú tong have been demolished in the last 30 years. Why?

4 Why are some hú tong kept as protected areas nowadays?

Birthdays

Traditionally, old people's birthdays are very important in China and are usually celebrated by the extended family getting together and having a big meal. In recent years, birthdays have become a more important occasion for the young too. Children get presents or money on their birthdays. They have parties or go out with friends for a meal. No matter whether old or young, the person whose birthday it is usually eats noodles because long noodles symbolise long life. Candles and cakes are becoming more popular as well.

汉字 hàn zì Investigating characters

Learning more about Chinese characters

WRITING 1 Copy the grid and choose one or two new characters from this chapter to fill in as the examples for each stroke.

Stroke	English name	Example character
一	Horizontal	有
丨	Vertical line	
丶	The dot	
丿	The sweeping left stroke	
乀	The sweeping right stroke	
乛	Turning stroke	

是　口　生　月　日　有　小　大　个

WRITING 2 Using characters from Activity 1, write them and their English translation next to the correct number of strokes.

Example: 2 strokes: 人 person

3 strokes

4 strokes

5 strokes

6 strokes

9 strokes

WRITING 3 Write an appropriate character for each gap.

我叫 Mingming, 我家有三 __1__ 人。

Christine 有一 __2__ 弟弟。

Nila 家 __3__ 五口 __4__ 。

我十 __5__ 岁。

我家有 __6__ 口 __7__ , 爸爸、妈妈和我。

我没 __8__ 哥哥、姐姐、弟弟、妹妹。

28 二十八

部首 bù shǒu **Radicals**

Radicals: 犭

Most characters with this radical are animals that live on land. For example, you have learned 猫 cat, and 狗 dog.

More examples are:

狼 láng = wolf   狮 shī = lion   猴 hóu = monkey   狐狸 hú li = fox

READING 4

Find the characters. How many are there of each animal?

狮　猫　狮　狮　猴　狼　狐狸　狗　狮
狗　狼　狼　狗　狮　狼　狐狸　猫

READING 5

Can you find these radicals in the characters which follow? Then match the characters to their meaning with the help of the radicals.

Example: **1 e** rock

1 石　stone   2 火　fire   3 舌　tongue
4 讠　speech   5 车　vehicle   6 饣　meal

a 饿   b 辆   c 甜   d 炒   e 岩   f 讲

rock   sweet   hungry   to talk/speak

to stir fry   measure word for bicycles/cars/coaches etc.

READING 6

Count the strokes of the radicals and put them in the correct order from the least to the most strokes.

1 石　stone   2 火　fire   3 舌　tongue
4 讠　speech   5 车　vehicle   6 饣　meal

Extension

1 Listen and write down what each person says about their pet and other information about their family or themselves. (1–6)

Example: 1 Liu Yihao: five fish. The family consists of Liu Yihao and his mum and dad.

1 Liu Yihao

2 Meko

3 Nadia

4 Zhao Yueming

5 Niu Huan

6 Katharine

2 Work in groups of 2–3 people to describe the people and pets from your answers to Activity 1.

3 Whose birthday is it?

___1___'s birthday is 25 March.

___2___'s birthday is 7 April.

___3___'s birthday is 3 September.

___4___'s birthday is 8 December.

___5___'s birthday is 30 June.

___6___'s birthday is 19 January.

a 妈妈的生日是六月三十日。

b 爸爸的生日是四月七日。

c 弟弟的生日是九月三日。

d 姐姐的生日是一月十九日。

e 哥哥的生日是十二月八日。

f 妹妹的生日是三月二十五日。

4 Choose the correct measure word to fill in the gap. Then translate the phrase or sentence into English.

Example: 一 _只_ 猫 one cat

三 __1__ 鱼

五 __2__ 蛇

我有四 __3__ 小狗。

哥哥有一 __4__ 大鸟。

我家有三 __5__ 人。

她有一 __6__ 弟弟。

a 个
b 只
c 条
d 口

30 三十

Chapter 2 家

READING 5 Spot the mistakes in the pictures according to the sentences.

1 我有四条蛇。

2 Anthony 有一条蛇，他没有猫和狗。

3 我家有四口人，我有爸爸、妈妈、一个姐姐。我有一只大狗。

4 我叫 Michael，我家有五口人，我有爸爸、妈妈、一个姐姐、一个妹妹。我家有一只猫、三只鸟。

Michael

SPEAKING 6 In pairs, introduce yourselves to each other. You can use the framework to help you.

我叫 ___ 。

我 ___ 岁。

我家有 ___ 口人。

我有 ___ (family member)。

我没有 ___ (family member)。

我有 ___ 只 / 条 ___ 。

我的生日是 ___ 。

WRITING 7 Write down the missing words.

我 _1_ Naomi，我 _2_ 四岁。我 _3_ 一只大猫。

我的生日是三 _4_ 十 _5_ 。

我家有四 _6_ 人，我有爸爸、妈妈和一 _7_ 弟弟。

我爸爸的生日 _8_ 九月十三日，我妈妈的 _9_ 是六月二十五日。

三十一 31

Review

I can:

①
- say who is in my family — 爸爸 bà ba, 妈妈 mā ma, 哥哥 gē ge, 姐姐 jiě jie, 弟弟 dì di, 妹妹 mèi mei
- use measure words 个 and 口 — 他有一个妹妹。 tā yǒu yí ge mèi mei / 我家有四口人。 wǒ jiā yǒu sì kǒu rén
- write key characters — 有、个、口、人

②
- say what pet I have/don't have — 我有一只猫。 wǒ yǒu yì zhī māo / 我没有狗。 wǒ méi yǒu gǒu
- use question word 吗 — 你有狗吗? nǐ yǒu gǒu ma
- use measure words 只 and 条 — 他有两只猫。 tā yǒu liǎng zhī māo / 她有四条鱼。 tā yǒu sì tiáo yú
- describe pets with adjectives 大 and 小 — 大狗 dà gǒu, 一只小猫 yì zhī xiǎo māo
- write key characters — 大、小

③
- say the date — 六月十七日 liù yuè shí qī rì / 十二月二十五日 shí èr yuè èr shí wǔ rì
- say when my birthday is — 我的生日是九月八日。 wǒ de shēng rì shì jiǔ yuè bā rì
- use the possessive adjective 的 — 我的生日 wǒ de shēng rì / 她的猫 tā de māo / 他的老师 tā de lǎo shī
- understand the date in characters — 六月十一日，我的生日是二月八日。
- write key characters — 日、月、是、生、日

Investigating characters

- count the number of strokes in a character — 人, 2 strokes
- recognise simple radicals — 犭

32 三十二

Test

Chapter 2 家

LISTENING 1 Listen and say whether the statements are true or false.

1. There are five people in the family.
2. Mum is 38 years old.
3. Rachel's birthday is 5 March.
4. The family has a dog.

SPEAKING 2 Pretend you are one of the children of the family in the picture. Introduce your family using the information provided.
You can use these phrases to help you:

我家有 ___ 口人。 wǒ jiā yǒu … kǒu rén

我有 ___ 。 wǒ yǒu …

我 ___ 岁。 wǒ … suì

___ 的生日是 ___ ___ 。 … de shēng rì shì …

我没有 ___ 。 wǒ méi yǒu …

Daniel — 5 March — 17 years old
Lily — 19 Feb — 8 years old
Harry — 1 July — 47 years old
Nicole — 8 Nov — 49 years old
Oscar — 26 Feb — 12 years old
Bubble — 6 April

READING 3 You have received an email from your Chinese penpal talking about her family. Read it and answer the questions in English.

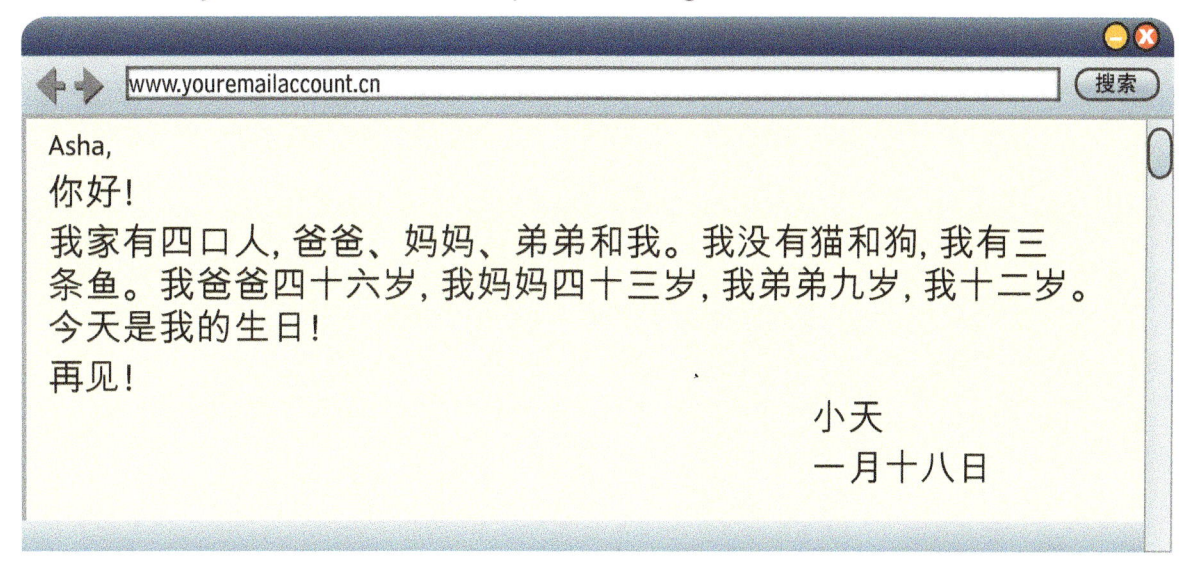

www.youremailaccount.cn 搜索

Asha,

你好!
我家有四口人,爸爸、妈妈、弟弟和我。我没有猫和狗,我有三条鱼。我爸爸四十六岁,我妈妈四十三岁,我弟弟九岁,我十二岁。今天是我的生日!
再见!

小天
一月十八日

1. How many people are there in Xiaotian's family?
2. How old are Xiaotian's mum and dad?
3. What pets does Xiaotian have?
4. What is the day special for?
5. When is Xiaotian's birthday?

WRITING 4 Write the characters for the English text.

1. month
2. date
3. 18 January
4. birthday
5. to be
6. to have
7. big
8. small

三十三 33

Key language

Family

爸爸	bà ba	dad	妹妹	mèi mei	younger sister
妈妈	mā ma	mum	家	jiā	home/family
哥哥	gē ge	older brother	有	yǒu	to have
姐姐	jiě jie	older sister	人	rén	person/people
弟弟	dì di	younger brother	口	kǒu	measure word for total number of family

Pets

狗	gǒu	dog	大	dà	big
猫	māo	cat	小	xiǎo	small
鸟	niǎo	bird	只	zhī	measure word for most animals and birds (cat, dog, bird, rabbit etc.)
鱼	yú	fish			
蛇	shé	snake	条	tiáo	measure word for long thin animals (snake, fish)
兔子	tù zi	rabbit			

Birthdays

一月	yī yuè	January	十月	shí yuè	October
二月	èr yuè	February	十一月	shí yī yuè	November
三月	sān yuè	March	十二月	shí èr yuè	December
四月	sì yuè	April	日	rì	date
五月	wǔ yuè	May	月	yuè	month
六月	liù yuè	June	生日	shēng rì	birthday
七月	qī yuè	July	今天	jīn tiān	today
八月	bā yuè	August	是	shì	to be
九月	jiǔ yuè	September			

Stroke order

有	一 ナ オ 冇 有 有
个	丿 𠆢 个
口	丨 冂 口
人	丿 人
大	一 ナ 大
小	亅 小 小
日	丨 冂 日 日
月	丿 冂 月 月
生	丿 ⺧ ⺧ 牛 生
是	是 是 是 是 旦 旦 昰 是

3 爱好 ài hào Hobbies

1 我们玩儿游戏吧! wǒ men wánr yóu xì ba Let's play games!

🌸 Talking about what you do in your free time

LISTENING 1 Listen to Li Yue talking about her family's hobbies. Match the family member with the correct hobby. (1–4)

爱好 ài hào hobby
你的爱好是什么？ nǐ de ài hào shì shén me
What is your hobby?

a 看书 kàn shū read books

b 听音乐 tīng yīn yuè listen to music

c 买东西 mǎi dōng xi go shopping

d 上网 shàng wǎng surf the Internet

Example: **1b**

1 妈妈   2 爸爸   3 妹妹   4 哥哥

LISTENING 2 Xiaoming is asking his new classmates about their hobbies. Listen and note down the letter of the correct picture from Activity 1. (1–4)

1 Zhang Xiaoli
2 Li Ying
3 Wang Tingting
4 Liu Xiaoyan

SPEAKING 3 In pairs, ask each other about hobbies and find the correct picture from Activity 1, then swap.

A: 你的爱好是什么？
nǐ de ài hào shì shén me

B: 我的爱好是上网。
wǒ de ài hào shì shàng wǎng

Culture
Chinese names

Chinese names are the other way round to English, with the surname first. For example, a man called Zhang Long has the surname Zhang and given name Long. The given name usually contains one or two Chinese characters. Chinese given names have particular meanings, which may express the parents' wishes for the newborn. Girls are often called 美 (měi, beautiful), 花 (huā, flower), 月 (yuè, moon); common names for boys include 明 (míng, bright), 强 (qiáng, strong), 龙 (lóng, dragon).

Grammar
The use of negatives

The negative of most verbs is made by adding 不 (bù) in front of the verb. For example:
我不上网。 I don't surf the Internet.
他不看书。 He doesn't read books.
(Remember, the verb is the same whether 'I' or 'he' is the subject of the sentence.)

36 三十六

Chapter 3 爱好

READING 4 Read the sentences and copy and complete the grid.

1. 你好！我叫 Kate, 我今天看书, 不上网。
2. 早上好！我叫 Sam, 我今天不听音乐, 我买东西。
3. 早上好！我叫 Lili, 今天我上网, 不看书。
4. 你好！我叫 Leena, 我今天不买东西, 我看书。
5. 我叫 Xiaodong, 今天我听音乐, 不上网。再见！

Grammar

Position of time words

In Chinese, the time when you do something comes before the verb, which means it is at the very beginning of a sentence or straight after the subject. This is different from English, in which the time is often put at the end of the sentence. For example, in English you say 'I'm not surfing the Internet today'. In Chinese you say 今天我不上网。or 我今天不上网。

Activities	Who does?	Who doesn't?
Read books	Kate, Leena	Lili
Surf the Internet		
Go shopping		
Listen to music		

READING 5 Choose the characters from the box to match the sentences below and translate the sentences into English.

Example: **a** = 1, 12, 5; I read books.

a 我看书。
b 你听音乐。
c 他上网。
d 妈妈看书。
e 爸爸不买东西。

1 我	2 乐	3 音	4 不
5 书	6 你	7 爸爸	8 东
9 西	10 妈妈	11 网	12 看
13 听	14 上	15 买	16 他

SPEAKING 6 In groups, pretend that you are from one family. Ask each other what you're going to do this morning.

A: 爸爸, 今天你上网吗？ bà ba jīn tiān nǐ shàng wǎng ma

B: 今天我上网/不上网。 jīn tiān wǒ shàng wǎng/bú shàng wǎng

WRITING 7 Practise writing the following key characters for this unit. Look at page 53 if you need more help with stroke order.

书　不　上　网

三十七　37

② 我喜欢看电视！ wǒ xǐ huan kàn diàn shì I like watching TV!

Talking about what you like doing

喜欢 xǐ huan to like
看电影 kàn diàn yǐng to watch films
看电视 kàn diàn shì to watch TV

玩儿电脑 游戏 wánr diàn nǎo yóu xì to play computer games
玩儿滑板 wánr huá bǎn to skateboard
你呢？ nǐ ne How about you?

LISTENING 1

A girl called Xiaojing and a boy called Wang Jian are talking about their hobbies.
Listen and note down the letters of the correct pictures.

Xiaojing likes __1__; dislikes __2__.   Wang Jian likes __3__; dislikes __4__.

a 看电影 kàn diàn yǐng 
b 看电视 kàn diàn shì 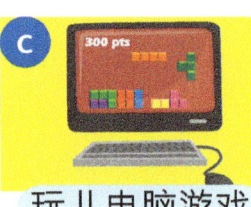
c 玩儿电脑游戏 wánr diàn nǎo yóu xì 
d 玩儿滑板 wánr huá bǎn

喜欢 xǐ huan
不喜欢 bù xǐ huan 

Grammar

The use of 也 yě

也 means 'also' or 'too'. Its position is always just before the verb in Chinese sentences – it is not as flexible as English. For example, 'I like watching TV, too.' in Chinese is 我也喜欢看电视。也 is placed between 我 and 喜欢.

SPEAKING 2

In pairs, take turns asking each other about what you like doing.

A: 我喜欢___/不喜欢___, 你呢？ wǒ xǐ huan…/bù xǐ huan… nǐ ne
B: 我也喜欢___/不喜欢___。 wǒ yě xǐ huan…/bù xǐ huan…

LISTENING 3

Listen to these people talking about things they like doing.
Match the name with the correct activity. (1–8)

Example: **1 d, e**

1 Li Dashan	5 Xiaodong	a watching TV	e listening to music
2 Lili	6 Zhang Mei	b reading books	f playing computer games
3 Xiaolong	7 Lele	c watching films	g going shopping
4 Zhang Xiaohua	8 Xiaoling	d surfing the Internet	h skateboarding

38 三十八

Chapter 3 爱好

READING 4 Read the sentences and copy and complete the grid.

我叫 Dayong, 我喜欢看电影, 不喜欢看书。
我叫 Zhang Long, 我喜欢上网, 不喜欢看电视。
我叫 Xiaoli, 我喜欢玩儿滑板, 不喜欢看电影。
我叫 Tingting, 我喜欢玩儿电脑游戏, 不喜欢买东西。
我叫 Li Ying, 我喜欢看电视, 不喜欢听音乐。
我叫 Daming, 我喜欢买东西, 不喜欢上网。
我叫 Xiaoyan, 我喜欢听音乐, 不喜欢玩儿电脑游戏。
我叫 Zhao Xiaojing, 我喜欢看书, 不喜欢玩儿滑板。

Pinyin

How to pronounce x

The x in pinyin is pronounced something like 'sh' as in 'she', but to say it perfectly, you must put your tongue behind your lower teeth. Listen and then try practising these words:

1. xǐ huan (喜欢, to like)
2. xīng xing (星星, star)
3. xià xuě (下雪, to snow)
4. xiè xie (谢谢, to thank)
5. xiàn zài (现在, now)

Activities	Who likes?	Who doesn't like?
Watching TV		
Reading		
Watching films		
Playing computer games		
Listening to music		
Going shopping		
Skateboarding		
Surfing the Internet		

WRITING 5 Practise writing the following key characters for this unit. Look at page 53 if you need more help with stroke order.

看 电 影 视 也

WRITING 6 Fill in the gaps with the correct characters according to the pictures.

1 Xiaoli 喜欢＿＿, 不喜欢＿＿。

2 Li Long 喜欢＿＿, 不喜欢＿＿。

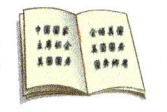

三十九 39

3 你会游泳吗? nǐ huì yóu yǒng ma — Can you swim?

Talking about sport

LISTENING 1 Listen and note down which sport each of the following five people likes and which they dislike. (1–5)

谁喜欢? shéi xǐ huan Who likes ...?

Example: 1 c a

1 Liu Jian — a
2 Wang Ping — b
3 Zhao Qing — c
4 Xiaohua — d
5 Dali — e
f

踢足球	打篮球	打乒乓球	打网球	跑步	游泳
tī zú qiú	dǎ lán qiú	dǎ pīng pāng qiú	dǎ wǎng qiú	pǎo bù	yóu yǒng

SPEAKING 2 In pairs, ask and answer questions about the people in Activity 1.

A: 谁喜欢游泳? shéi xǐ huan yóu yǒng

B: Dali 喜欢游泳。 dali xǐ huan yóu yǒng

A: 谁不喜欢打网球? shéi bù xǐ huan dǎ wǎng qiú

B: Xiaohua 不喜欢打网球。 xiaohua bù xǐ huan dǎ wǎng qiú

Grammar

The use of 谁 shéi **, who..?**

谁 can be used at the beginning or end of a question, wherever the answer to 'Who?' is required. When you use question words like this in Chinese, you don't have to change the word order as you do in English. You answer by taking out the question word and replacing it with the answer. For example:

他是谁? Who is he? (literally, 'He is who?')
他是我哥哥。 He is my elder brother.
谁喜欢看书? Who likes reading?
小明喜欢看书。 Xiaoming likes reading.

LISTENING 3 Listen to and read the sentences; then copy and complete the table. (1–5)

1 我叫丽丽,我十五岁。
我会游泳,不会打球。

2 我叫李明,我十二岁。
我会踢足球,不会打乒乓球。

3 我叫兰兰,我十一岁。
我会打篮球,不会打网球。

4 我叫小强,我十三岁。
我会打乒乓球,不会游泳。

5 我叫张玲,我十四岁。
我会打网球,我不会踢足球。

Name	Age	Can ...	Can't ...
1 Lili	15	Swim	Play ball games
2 Li Ming			
3 Lanlan			
4 Xiaoqiang			
5 Zhang Ling			

会 huì to know how to
打球 dǎ qiú to play ball games
运动 yùn dòng sport

40 四十

Chapter 3 爱好

Grammar

The use of 会 huì = can
(to know how to do something)

The verb 会 refers to a skill rather than being physically able to do something. To make the negative, you just put 不 in front of 会. For example:

我会打网球，不会打乒乓球。
wǒ huì dǎ wǎng qiú, bú huì dǎ pīng pāng qiú
I can play tennis. I can't play table tennis.

Pinyin

How to pronounce -ong

You have learned 游泳 (yóu yǒng) and 运动 (yùn dòng) in this chapter. Be careful: the -ong sound in pinyin is not pronounced as you might think. Listen and then try practising these words.
1 yóu yǒng (游泳, swim)
2 yùn dòng (运动, sport)
3 yǒng yuǎn (永远, forever)
4 zhōng wǔ (中午, noon)
5 gōng rén (工人, worker)

SPEAKING 4 Class survey. How many people in your class like sport and can play these sports? Make a chart for your answers.
Don't forget to include measure words!

A: 你喜欢运动吗？ nǐ xǐ huan yùn dòng ma
B: 我喜欢/不喜欢运动。 wǒ xǐ huan / bù xǐ huan yùn dòng
A: 你会踢足球吗？ nǐ huì tī zú qiú ma
B: 我会踢足球 / 我不会踢足球。 wǒ huì tī zú qiú / wǒ bú huì tī zú qiú

READING 5 Match the speech bubbles with the correct sportsperson.

a b c d e

1 我会游泳，我喜欢游泳。
2 我会打乒乓球，我喜欢打乒乓球。
3 我会打篮球，我喜欢打篮球。
4 我会踢足球，我喜欢踢足球。
5 我会打网球，我喜欢打网球。

WRITING 6 Practise writing the following key characters for this unit. Remember: left to right and top to bottom. Look at page 53 for more help with stroke order.

| 打 | 喜 | 欢 | 会 | 球 |

WRITING 7 Write the following sentences in Chinese.
(You don't have to write the characters for the names.)

1 Meimei likes watching films.
2 Xiaoming doesn't like reading.
3 Dabao can play ball games.

四十一 41

4 我星期一上网 wǒ xīng qī yī shàng wǎng — I surf the net on Mondays

❀ Learning the days of the week

1 Listen and repeat the days of the week.

六月

星期一	星期二	星期三	星期四	星期五	星期六	星期日
			1	2	3	4
5	6	7	8	9	10	11
12	13	15	16	17	18	

星期一	xīng qī yī	Monday
星期二	xīng qī èr	Tuesday
星期三	xīng qī sān	Wednesday
星期四	xīng qī sì	Thursday
星期五	xīng qī wǔ	Friday
星期六	xīng qī liù	Saturday
星期日	xīng qī rì	Sunday

2 Read Lili's diary and answer the questions.

丽丽 — lì li — a girl's name
记事本 — jì shì běn — diary

记事本

丽丽的记事本
星期一：上网
星期二：打乒乓球
星期三：打网球
星期四：看电视
星期五：听音乐
星期六：看电影
星期日：踢足球

1 On which day does Lili listen to music?
2 On which day does Lili play table tennis?
3 On which day does Lili watch TV?
4 On which day does Lili play tennis?
5 On which day does Lili watch films?

3 In pairs, using Activity 2, ask and answer questions about Lili's diary.

A: Lili 星期六看电影吗？
   lili xīng qī liù kàn diàn yǐng ma
B: Lili 星期六看电影。
   lili xīng qī liù kàn diàn yǐng

Language

Days of the week

It is easy to say the days of the week in Chinese. Starting with Monday, you just put 一 after 星期 (xīng qī, week); 星期二 for Tuesday; and so on. The only different one is Sunday, which doesn't use a number: it's 星期日 or 星期天. You use 天 (tiān) more often when you are talking, but you might see 日 more in a book or newspaper.

Pinyin

Pronouncing qi

Although this sound is written as qi in pinyin, it is actually pronounced a bit like 'chee' as in 'cheese'. Listen and then practise the rhyme below:

一 二 三 四 五 六 七，七 六 五
yī èr sān sì wǔ liù qī qī liù wǔ

四 三 二 一。
sì sān èr yī

七 个 阿 姨 来 摘 果，七 只 篮
qī ge ā yí lái zhāi guǒ qī zhī lán

子 手 中 提。
zi shǒu zhōng tí

七 种 果 子 摆 七 样：苹 果、
qī zhǒng guǒ zi bǎi qī yàng píng guǒ

桃 子、石 榴、柿 子、李 子、
táo zi   shí liu   shì zi   lǐ zi

栗 子、梨。
lì zi   lí

42 四十二

Chapter 3 爱好

4 Listen and note down which day Xiaohai does the following sports.

Example: swimming – Tuesday

play football

play table tennis

running

play basketball

play tennis

skateboard

这个星期 zhè ge xīng qī this week

5 Practise writing the key characters for this unit. Remember: left to right and top to bottom. Look at page 53 if you need more help with stroke order.

星 期

6 Mingming and Lili are talking about the sports they're doing this week. Listen, then copy and complete the table in English.

	星期一	星期二	星期三	星期四	星期五	星期六	星期日
Lili	play basketball						
Mingming							

7 Look at Activity 2 and write down which day Lili does the following activities:

Example: a 星期二

四十三 43

⑤ 年轻人的爱好 nián qīng rén de ài hào   Young people's hobbies

Learning about young people's hobbies in China

网络 wǎng luò the Internet

The Internet is just as popular with young people in China as it is in the UK. Internet cafes are widely used and can be an escape from the 'real world'. 'QQ' is the most popular online chat service, similar to MSN or Skype. Many young people, especially in cities, also have computers at home. They chat with friends and play games online as well as use educational sites. There are quite a lot of websites to help students with their schoolwork. However, Chinese secondary school students don't usually use computers to do their homework. They are always encouraged to write their homework on paper so that they don't forget how to write Chinese characters, as well as the English they are learning!

电视 diàn shì TV

Chinese TV in the cities has many channels, sometimes over 100 to choose from. Television series are popular; there are many different types which usually have between 20 and 50 episodes. 古装戏 (gǔ zhuāng xì, costume dramas) are set in ancient China with elaborate traditional costumes; modern dramas that deal with many modern issues such as 《奋斗》 (fèn dòu, "Struggle") and 《我的青春谁做主》 (wǒ de qīng chūn shéi zuò zhǔ, "My Youth") are very successful. Recently, singing and talent show competitions such as 《超级女声》 (chāo jí nǚ shēng, "Super Girls") have gained large numbers of young viewers who support their favourites. The Taiwan comic entertainment show 《康熙来了》 (kāng xī lái le, "Here Comes Kangxi") where celebrities are interviewed and 'grilled', and music channels such as Channel V are also watched by lots of young people.

运动 yùn dòng Sport

Basketball is by far the most popular sport for young people in many parts of China; it is played in schools as well as for fun. Table tennis, skating, badminton and football are also popular, and the first two are often practised in public parks. Many young people are football and basketball fans who follow international games, and some even get up in the middle of the night to watch live games. Primary and secondary school pupils enjoy skipping ropes and kicking Chinese shuttlecocks, which are fun activities that can be played alone or together in a group, and are good for keeping fit.

Chapter 3 爱好

卡拉OK kǎ lā OK **Karaoke**

Karaoke is one of the most popular pastimes for young people in China. They often have karaoke parties for their birthdays, and some people practise by themselves in order to brush up their singing skills and impress friends. Karaoke's popularity reflects young people's love of listening to pop music on their music players, online and on TV. Someone who won't let go of the microphone and let someone else have a go is called a 'mài bà' (麦霸), literally a 'microphone controller'.

出去玩儿, 出去吃 chū qù wánr chū qù chī **Going out and eating out**

Just like here, young people like to go shopping in large shopping malls or in smaller markets where items can be haggled for. Street basketball, where you have to make a number of successful shots within a time limit, and Dance Revolution, where you stand on a dancing mat or platform and dance to the patterns on screen, can often be found in squares and large shopping centres.

Just as for older people, eating out remains very popular with young people. Friends go together to enjoy all kinds of food, which is usually much less expensive in China than in many western countries. Apart from delicious Chinese regional cuisines such as Cantonese, Sichuan and Shandong, food from outside China such as pizza, curry and sushi, along with KFC and McDonalds, is very popular with young people.

READING 1 Match the verbs and the nouns to make five hobbies. Then translate the phrases into English.

1 唱　　　　　　　a 电视
2 看　　　　　　　b 运动
3 上　　　　　　　c 电脑游戏
4 玩儿　　　　　　d 网
5 做　　　　　　　e 卡拉OK

年轻人 nián qīng rén young people
做 zuò to do
唱 chàng to sing
卡拉OK kǎ lā OK karaoke

READING 2 Do some more research into the activities mentioned above. Split into groups to look at different topics.

- Try to relate your research to young people and make a group presentation to the class using PowerPoint if possible.

- You could put the information you find into graphs and label them in Chinese.

四十五 45

汉字 hàn zì Investigating characters

❀ Learning more about Chinese characters

One way of remembering Chinese characters is to make up stories about them which make sense to you. Some Chinese words may share a character because their meanings are related.

看 kàn

The same Chinese character is used for 'look', 'watch', 'see' and 'read'. They are all 看 kàn, as they all have something to do with eyes. The top part of the character 看 is 手 (shǒu, hand) while the bottom is 目 (mù, eye). It is like someone looking into the distance while hiding his eyes from the sunshine with a hand.

电 diàn

The Chinese words for computer, television and film share the character 电. Computer, television and film in Chinese are literally 'electric brain' 电脑, 'electric vision' 电视 and 'electric shadow' 电影. 电 consists of two parts: 曰 and 乚.

WRITING 1 Use the new characters you have learnt from this chapter to make five sentences. You will need to use other characters you already know. See page 53 for the new characters from this chapter.

WRITING 2 Read Grace's blog and write what she's doing this week in Chinese. Use full sentences.

Example:
Grace星期一买东西。

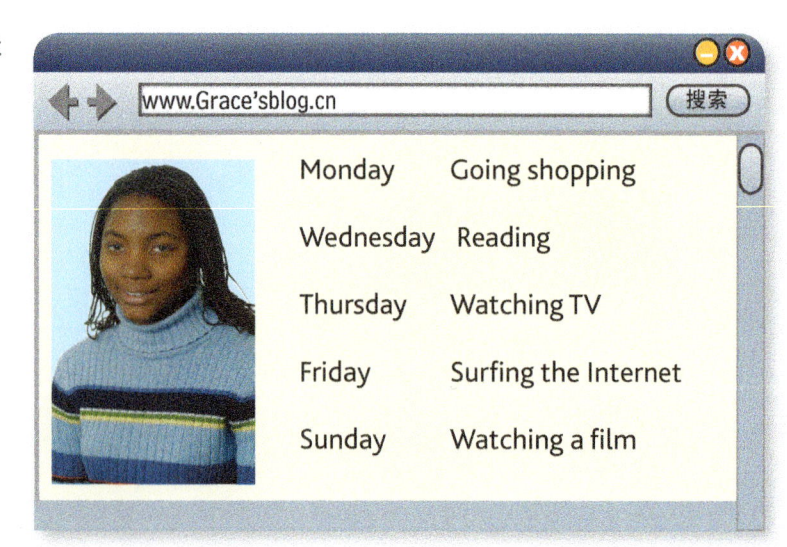

www.Grace'sblog.cn   搜索

Monday	Going shopping
Wednesday	Reading
Thursday	Watching TV
Friday	Surfing the Internet
Sunday	Watching a film

46 四十六

部首 bù shǒu **Radicals**

扌 and 氵

One of the advantages of learning Chinese radicals is that they will help you to remember characters. You will also need to know radicals in order to use a Chinese dictionary.

扌

The radical 扌 comes from the character 手 (shǒu, hand). If a character has this radical it usually means an action with a hand. For example, 提 (tí) = to lift, to carry; 把 (bǎ) = to hold. Interestingly, the character 打 (dǎ) has many meanings in Chinese: 'to hit', 'to beat', 'to play', 'to make', 'to open': 打网球, 打乒乓球, etc. However, if you say 'play football' in Chinese, you say 踢足球 (tī zú qiú, kick football) because you play football with feet (足), not hands!

氵

The radical 氵 represents three drops of water. Characters with this radical are usually related to water. For example, 游 (yóu, to swim), 河 (hé, river), 汗 (hàn, sweat).

READING 3 Translate the sentences below. Be careful with the meaning of 看.

1 你看!

2 我去 (qù, go) 看姐姐。

3 他喜欢看书。

4 她今天不看电视。

READING 4 Using the radicals, match the Chinese with the English words.

1	电话	a	to clean
2	打扫	b	grandmother
3	海洋	c	eyebrow
4	眼眉	d	shout
5	奶奶	e	telephone
6	呼喊	f	sea

Extension

1 Listen to a conversation between a girl called Xiaoli and a boy called Xiaoming and say whether the statements are true or false.

1. The two people are talking about hobbies.
2. Xiaoming doesn't like reading.
3. Xiaoli likes surfing the Internet.
4. Xiaoming also likes surfing the Internet.
5. Xiaoli likes watching films.
6. Neither Xiaoming nor Xiaoli likes listening to music.

2 In pairs, use the examples below to ask and answer each other's questions.

A: 你喜欢 ___ 吗？

B: 我喜欢/不喜欢 ___ 。

A: 你会 ___ 吗？

B: 我会/不会 ___ 。

A: 星期 ___ ，你 ___ 吗？

B: 星期 ___ ，我 ___ 。

3 Read the text and answer the questions in English.

他叫王大明，他喜欢玩儿电脑游戏，不喜欢看电视。他会打乒乓球，不会打网球。他星期五游泳，星期日看电影。

1. What does Wang Daming like/dislike doing?
2. What can/can't he do?
3. What does he do on Fridays?
4. Which day does he watch films?

48　四十八

Chapter 3 爱好

WRITING 4 Fill in the gaps, replacing the English in brackets with the correct Chinese.

1 我喜欢 (surfing the Internet)，不喜欢 (reading)。
2 爸爸 (on Thursday) 打球，(on Saturday) 跑步。
3 妈妈 (likes) 看电视，(doesn't like) 看电影。
4 哥哥 (can) 踢足球，(can't) 游泳。

READING 5 Read the email about Mei Ying's family and choose the correct answer for each question.

和 hé + *someone* +
一起 yì qǐ = together
去 qù to go

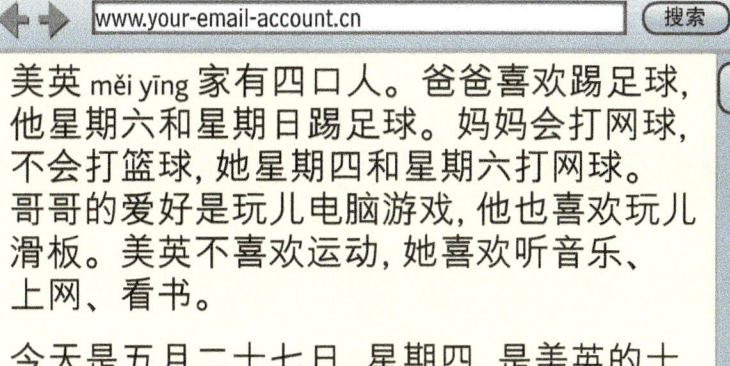

www.your-email-account.cn   搜索

美英 měi yīng 家有四口人。爸爸喜欢踢足球，他星期六和星期日踢足球。妈妈会打网球，不会打篮球，她星期四和星期六打网球。哥哥的爱好是玩儿电脑游戏，他也喜欢玩儿滑板。美英不喜欢运动，她喜欢听音乐、上网、看书。

今天是五月二十七日，星期四，是美英的十六岁生日。今天，她和家人一起去听音乐、看电影，他们也一起去买书。

1 谁喜欢踢足球？   a 爸爸   b 妈妈   c 哥哥
2 妈妈会打篮球吗？   a 会   b 不会
3 谁星期六打网球？   a 爸爸   b 妈妈   c 哥哥
4 哥哥喜欢玩儿什么？   a 篮球   b 足球   c 滑板
5 美英喜欢打球吗？   a 喜欢   b 不喜欢
6 她的生日是星期日吗？ a 是   b 不是
7 她多大？   a 十五   b 十六   c 十七
8 她今天听音乐吗？   a 听   b 不听
9 她和家人去买什么？   a 书   b 电脑   c 网球

四十九 49

Review

I can:

1
- say some hobbies — 看书 kàn shū, 买东西 mǎi dōng xi, 上网 shàng wǎng, 听音乐 tīng yīn yuè
- ask and answer about hobbies — 你的爱好是什么？nǐ de ài hào shì shén me, 我的爱好是上网。wǒ de ài hào shì shàng wǎng
- use the negative — 不 bù
- say what I and other people don't do — 不上网 bú shàng wǎng, 不听音乐 bù tīng yīn yuè
- write new characters — 书、不、上、网

2
- say some more hobbies — 看电影/电视 kàn diàn yǐng/diàn shì, 玩儿电脑游戏 wánr diàn nǎo yóu xì, 玩儿滑板 wánr huá bǎn
- tell people what I like/dislike doing — 我喜欢看电视。wǒ xǐ huan kàn diàn shì 我喜欢玩儿电脑游戏。wǒ xǐ huan wánr diàn nǎo yóu xì
- ask and answer questions about likes and dislikes — 你喜欢看书吗？我喜欢看书。你喜欢上网吗？我不喜欢上网。
- use the particle 呢 — 我喜欢看书，你呢？wǒ xǐ huan kàn shū nǐ ne
- understand the position of 也 — 我也喜欢看电视。wǒ yě xǐ huan kàn diàn shì
- write new characters — 看、电、影、视、也

3
- say some sports in Chinese — 踢足球 tī zú qiú, 打篮球 dǎ lán qiú, 打乒乓球 dǎ pīng pāng qiú, 打网球 dǎ wǎng qiú, 跑步 pǎo bù, 游泳 yóu yǒng
- use the question word 'Who?' — 谁 shéi
- say what I can or can't do — 会/不会 huì/bú huì
- ask people what they can do — 你会打篮球吗？
- write new characters — 打、喜欢、会、球

4
- say the days of the week — 星期一/二/三/四/五/六/日 xīng qī yī, etc.
- understand the position of time words — 星期一我踢足球 or 我星期一踢足球。
- tell people what I do during the week — 我星期一打篮球，星期二游泳…
- ask people if they do a hobby on a particular day of a week — 你星期日看电视吗？我星期日看电视。
- write new characters — 星、期

Investigating characters
- recognise some radicals in characters — 目、扌、氵

50　五十

Test

Chapter 3 爱好

LISTENING 1 A girl called Xiaoying and a boy called Dawei are talking about their hobbies. Listen and choose the right answer for each question. (1–6)

Example: **1b**

1	Who likes listening to music?	a Dawei	b Xiaoying
2	Which activity do both of them dislike?	a shopping	b watching TV
3	Which activity can both of them do?	a computer games	b skateboarding
4	Who can't play basketball?	a Xiaoying	b Dawei
5	What do both of them do on Saturday?	a tennis	b football
6	Who plays computer games on Sunday?	a Xiaoying	b Dawei

SPEAKING 2 Ask and answer the questions in Chinese with your partner.

1 你叫什么？ nǐ jiào shén me
2 你多大？ nǐ duō dà
3 你家有几口人？ nǐ jiā yǒu jǐ kǒu rén
4 你喜欢…吗？ nǐ xǐ huan … ma
5 你会…吗？ nǐ huì … ma

READING 3 Match the Chinese to the pictures.

Example: **1d**

1 打网球   2 看书   3 买东西   4 看电视   5 打篮球   6 游泳   7 跑步

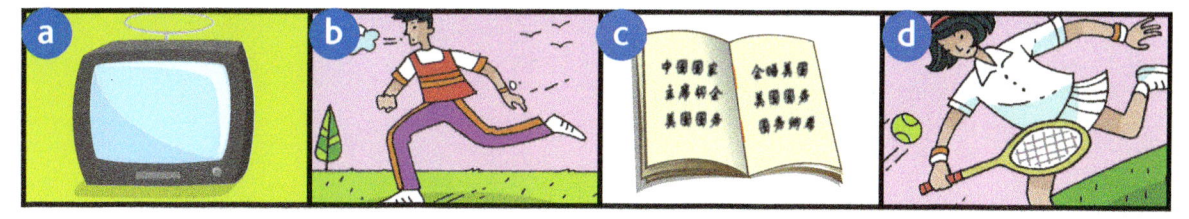

WRITING 4 Translate the following sentences into Chinese.

1 Sam likes reading and doesn't like surfing the Internet.
2 Xiaoming can't play ball games.
3 Dawei watches TV on Thursday and watches films on Saturday.

五十一 51

Key language

Hobbies

你的爱好是什么?	nǐ de ài hào shì shén me	What is your hobby?	玩儿电脑游戏	wánr diàn nǎo yóu xì	to play computer games
看书	kàn shū	to read	玩儿滑板	wánr huá bǎn	to skateboard
听音乐	tīng yīn yuè	to listen to music	喜欢	xǐ huan	to like
买东西	mǎi dōng xi	to go shopping	不喜欢	bù xǐ huan	to dislike
上网	shàng wǎng	to surf the Internet	你呢?	nǐ ne	How about you?
看电影	kàn diàn yǐng	to watch films	也	yě	also, too
看电视	kàn diàn shì	to watch TV			

Sports

谁	shéi	Who ...?	打网球	dǎ wǎng qiú	to play tennis
运动	yùn dòng	sport	跑步	pǎo bù	to run
踢足球	tī zú qiú	to play football	游泳	yóu yǒng	to swim
打篮球	dǎ lán qiú	to play basketball	打球	dǎ qiú	to play ball games
打乒乓球	dǎ pīng pāng qiú	to play table tennis	会	huì	can (do something skilled)

Days of the week

星期一	xīng qī yī	Monday	星期五	xīng qī wǔ	Friday
星期二	xīng qī èr	Tuesday	星期六	xīng qī liù	Saturday
星期三	xīng qī sān	Wednesday	星期日	xīng qī rì	Sunday
星期四	xīng qī sì	Thursday			

Stroke order

书	乛 乊 书 书
不	一 アイ 不
上	丨 上 上
网	丨 冂 冈 冈 网 网
看	一 二 三 手 看 看 看 看
电	丨 冂 曰 曰 电
影	日 曰 昌 景 景 景 景 昌 昌 景 景 景 影 影 影
视	丶 冫 衤 礻 礻 视 视 视
也	乛 也 也
打	一 十 扌 打 打
喜	一 十 吉 吉 吉 吉 吉 壴 喜 喜 喜
欢	乛 又 欢 欢 欢 欢
会	丿 人 会 会 会 会
球	一 王 王 王 玗 玗 玗 球 球 球
星	丨 冂 曰 曰 旦 早 星 星
期	一 十 廿 廿 其 其 其 期 期 期 期

4 学校 xué xiào School

1 中文很酷! zhōng wén hěn kù Chinese is cool!

Talking about school subjects

LISTENING 1

Listen to five people talking about their school subjects. Note down the letter of the correct picture. (1–5)

Example: Zhang Xiuli: **h, d**

1. Zhang Xiuli
2. Wang Yongqing
3. Li Yuling
4. Liu Chunming
5. Zhao Xiaochuan

学校 xué xiào school

学 xué to learn

课 kè lesson

你喜欢什么课? nǐ xǐ huan shén me kè
What lessons do you like?

a 中文 zhōng wén
b 英文 yīng wén
c 法文 fǎ wén
d 德文 dé wén
e 科学 kē xué
f 数学 shù xué
g 历史 lì shǐ
h 地理 dì lǐ
i 体育 tǐ yù
j 音乐 yīn yuè

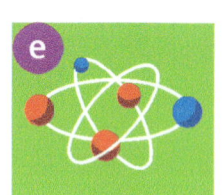

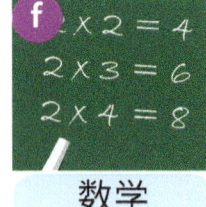

LISTENING 2

Xiaolong is talking about the lessons he has each morning. Note down the letter of the correct picture from Activity 1.

小龙的课 Xiaolong's lessons

星期一	星期二	星期三	星期四	星期五
f, b, g				

Pinyin

How to pronounce the vowel 'e' in pinyin

To make the 'e' sound in Chinese, make a sound as if you have seen something really disgusting: ergh! When 'e' is used with other vowels, it is pronounced like the 'e' in the English word 'bed'. Now listen and practise the pinyin below:

1. è (饿, hungry) chē (车, vehicle) kè (课, lesson)
2. běi (北, north) lěng (冷, cold) xué (学, learn)
3. biǎn biǎn zuǐ, ē ē ē   dà bái é, é é é   zhēn ě xīn, ě ě ě   wǒ è le, è è è
   扁扁嘴, ē ē ē   大白鹅, é é é   真恶心, ě ě ě   我饿了, è è è

54 五十四

Chapter 4 学校

Grammar

The use of 什么 shén me

As you've already seen, the question word 什么 is usually put at the end of the sentence and means 'what?' Sometimes a noun (such as 'book', 'person', 'lesson') follows it; this makes the question more specific. Look at these examples:

你喜欢什么？ = You like what? (The answer could be anything.)
你喜欢什么课？ = You like what **lesson**? (Here the answer must be a lesson; it is not a question about your favourite hobby! A possible answer might be 我喜欢数学课。 = I like maths.)

SPEAKING 3 Interview five classmates. Ask them what lessons they like and dislike, using the example to help you. Record your results in a chart like the one below and then report your results in Chinese to the class.

A: 你喜欢什么课？ nǐ xǐ huan shén me kè
B: 我喜欢中文课和历史课。 wǒ xǐ huan zhōng wén kè hé lì shǐ kè
A: 你不喜欢什么课？ nǐ bù xǐ huan shén me kè
B: 我不喜欢英文课和数学课。 wǒ bù xǐ huan yīng wén kè hé shù xué kè

(name) 名字	👍	👎
Amy	Chinese, history	English, maths

Example: Amy 喜欢中文课和历史课。她不喜欢英文课和数学课。

READING 4 Read the sentences and note down which day each person has each subject.

Example: Zhang Ling 星期一 science, 星期三 history

1 我叫 Zhang Ling, 我喜欢科学课和历史课。我星期一有科学课, 星期三有历史课。
2 你好！我叫 Leo。我喜欢中文课和数学课。我星期二有中文课, 星期四有数学课。
3 我叫 Xiaodong, 我喜欢音乐课, 也喜欢英文课。我星期一有音乐课, 星期四有英文课。
4 我叫 Li Yue, 我喜欢地理课和德文课。我星期三有地理课, 星期五有德文课。
5 你好！我是 Rohan。我喜欢法文课, 也喜欢体育课。我星期二有法文课, 星期五有体育课。

WRITING 5 Practise writing the following key characters for this unit and then write the phrases 'to learn Chinese' and 'to learn English' in Chinese. Remember: left falling before right falling.

中 文 学 英 课

WRITING 6 Translate these sentences into Chinese. Don't worry about translating the names.

1 Lisa doesn't surf the Internet.
2 Jenny learns Chinese on Monday.
3 Li Dongqing likes English lessons.

五十五 55

② 你几点上课? nǐ jǐ diǎn shàng kè — What time's your class?

🌸 Telling the time

READING 1 Match the times to the correct clock.

Example: **1a**

1. 上午九点
2. 下午两点半
3. 上午十点二十分
4. 下午三点四十分
5. 下午一点半
6. 上午十一点十五分

点 diǎn o'clock
分 fēn minute
半 bàn half
上午 shàng wǔ morning
下午 xià wǔ afternoon
节 jié a measure word for lessons
几点? jǐ diǎn What time?

Grammar

The use of 几 jǐ

几 means 'How many?' or 'How much?'. It is always used with a measure word and when expecting a low number (10 or less) in reply. Its place in a question depends on where the answer is going to be. For example:

A: 今天星期几? jīn tiān xīng qī jǐ What day of the week is it today?
B: 今天星期五。 jīn tiān xīng qī wǔ It is Friday today.
A: 你家有几口人? nǐ jiā yǒu jǐ kǒu rén How many people are there in your family?
B: 四口人。 sì kǒu rén Four people.

LISTENING 2 Listen to a boy called Lin Dongming and a girl called Yu Hongxia talking about their lessons. Answer the questions in English.

1. What lessons does Yu Hongxia have today?
2. What time does Yu Hongxia have a science lesson?
3. Which day does Yu Hongxia have a Chinese lesson?
4. What time does Lin Dongming have a French lesson?
5. What time does Lin Dongming have a music lesson?

SPEAKING 3 In pairs, one person says a time and the other chooses the correct clock. Then swap.

Example:

A: 上午十点。
B: b

56 五十六

Chapter 4 学校

Grammar

The order of time words

The order of time words in a Chinese sentence is always from the least specific (the month, the day of the week, etc.) to the most specific (the time). For example:

我星期一上午十点有体育课。 (literally: I Monday morning 10 have PE.)
我星期日下午四点半打篮球。 (I Sunday afternoon 4.30 play basketball.)

READING 4 Read the paragraph and note down the times and the lessons in English.

Example: 9am English

今天是星期五，我有五节课。上午九点，是英文课；十点十分，是数学课；十一点半，是体育课。下午一点二十分，是历史课；三点十五分，是科学课。四点十五分，我和哥哥有游泳课。

Grammar

The use of 是 shì

是 can be translated into English as 'is/am/are/be/been/being'. In English, you say 'I am a teacher', 'He is a teacher' and 'We are teachers', but in Chinese you use 是 in all three sentences: 我是老师。他是老师。我们是老师。

WRITING 5 Practise writing the following key characters for this unit. Remember: left to right and top to bottom.

上　下　午　点　分

WRITING 6 Fill in the gaps with the correct characters according to the pictures.

小明 _1_ 有 _2_ 课。　　大山 _3_ 有 _4_ 课。

SPEAKING 7 In pairs, ask and answer questions about subjects you study at school and what time you have them.

A: 你几点有音乐课？ nǐ jǐ diǎn yǒu yīn yuè kè
B: 我下午两点有音乐课。 wǒ xià wǔ liǎng diǎn yǒu yīn yuè kè

五十七 57

③ 我的课程表 wǒ de kè chéng biǎo — My timetable

Talking about your school timetable

LISTENING 1 Listen to Wang Lan talking to Li Yong about her new timetable. Complete her timetable in English; not all the gaps will be filled.

你们 nǐ men you (plural)
我们 wǒ men we

王兰的课程表

		星期一	星期二	星期三	星期四	星期五
上午	8:00	科学	中文	数学	地理	数学
	9:10	英文	数学	科学	数学	
	10:20			中文	历史	中文
	11:30		英文			体育
下午	2:10	美术		体育	英文	
	3:15	中文	电脑		法文	
	4:20	地理		英文		

Grammar

Making plural pronouns

Making plural pronouns (they, we, etc.) is easy in Chinese. You just add 们 (men) to the singular pronoun.

Singular	我 I	他 he	她 she	你 you
Plural	我们 we	他们 they (all male or mixed)	她们 they (all female)	你们 you

SPEAKING 2 In pairs, ask and answer questions about the completed timetable for Activity 1. Use the example below to help you.

A: 星期一上午八点，你有什么课？
xīng qī yī shàng wǔ bā diǎn, nǐ yǒu shén me kè

B: 我有科学课。 wǒ yǒu kē xué kè

Language

Saying 'yes' and 'no'

There is no single word for 'yes' or 'no' in Chinese. If someone asks you a question, you just repeat the verb (the action) and make it positive or negative. Look at these examples:

你是老师吗？不是，我是学生。
你喜欢看书吗？喜欢。
你今天有中文课吗？有 / 没有。

(remember that the negative is usually 不, except with 有 where it is 没).

58 五十八

Chapter 4 学校

READING 3

Read the passage below and choose the correct answers.

我们的星期一

你们好！我叫小星，我是哥哥。她叫小月，她是妹妹。我和小月星期一上午八点半上学。我十点十五分有数学课，小月有地理课；我十一点三十五分有体育课，小月有科学课；我们十二点吃午饭。我下午两点半有音乐课，小月有英文课。我们四点放学。我喜欢音乐课，小月喜欢地理课。你们喜欢什么课？

1 They go to school at	a 8.30	b 8.45
2 At 10.15, Xiaoxing has a	a geography lesson	b maths lesson
3 At 11.35, Xiaoyue has a	a PE lesson	b science lesson
4 They have lunch at	a 12.00	b 1pm
5 At 2.30pm, Xiaoxing has a	a music lesson	b geography lesson
6 at 4pm, they	a finish classes	b have a music lesson

上学 shàng xué to go to school

放学 fàng xué to finish classes and leave school

吃 chī to eat

午饭 wǔ fàn lunch

Pinyin

How to pronounce the vowel 'u'

Push your lips forward and make a small circle through which your breath can vibrate. Your lips should take the shape they make when you say the word 'fool'. Practise with a word you already know: 书 shū book

Now listen and practise a nursery rhyme:

小 枕 头 ， 胖 乎 乎 ， 让 我 枕 着 打 呼 噜 。
xiāo zhěn tóu　pàng hū hū　　ràng wǒ zhěn zhe dǎ hū lu

A small, fat pillow, let me rest my head on it and sleep, snoring.

呼 噜 噜 ， 呼 噜 噜 ， 好 像 枕 着 小 肥 猪 。
hū lū lū　　hū lū lū　　　hǎo xiàng zhěn zhe xiǎo féi zhū

Zzzzzzzz zzzzzzz. It is as if there is a small, fat pig under my head.

WRITING 4

Practise writing the following key characters for this unit. Remember: left to right and top to bottom.

我　你　们

WRITING 5

Your Chinese penfriend is visiting and is going to attend your Chinese and English lessons. Write down the days and times for him/her in Chinese.

Example 星期一下午三点有中文课。

1 Monday 3pm Chinese
2 Tuesday 9am English
3 Wednesday 2pm Chinese
4 Thursday 11 am English
5 Friday 10am Chinese

五十九 59

4 你们班大不大? nǐ men bān dà bu dà — Is your class big?

Talking about school in China

READING 1 Match the Chinese phrases with the English. Use the box on the right to help you

Example: 1 e

1. 男学生
2. 女学生
3. 我们班
4. 多少学生
5. 中国人
6. 英国人

a our class
b British person
c female students
d Chinese person
e male students
f how many students

男 nán male
女 nǚ female
学生 xué sheng student
班 bān class
多少 duō shǎo how many/how much
中国 zhōng guó China
英国 yīng guó Britain

LISTENING 2 Zhang Dazhong is being interviewed about his school. Listen to and read the interview then choose the correct answer for each question.

Interviewer:	张大中,你好! 你是英国人吗?
张大中:	不是,我不是英国人,我是中国人。
Interviewer:	你是学生吗?
张大中:	是,我是学生。
Interviewer:	你们班有多少学生?
张大中:	我们班有二十三个学生。有十二个女学生,十一个男学生。
Interviewer:	你们几点上学? 几点放学?
张大中:	我们上午八点上学,下午四点半放学。

Grammar

Nationality

To say your nationality in Chinese, say your country's name first followed by 人 rén 'person'.
For example:
Chinese: 中国人 ('China' + 'person' = Chinese)
British: 英国人 ('Britain' + 'person' = British)

1 Zhang Dazhong's nationality is — a Chinese   b British
2 How many female students in his class?   a 11   b 12
3 How many male students in his class?   a 11   b 12
4 What time does he go to school?   a 8.00   b 8.30
5 What time does he finish school?   a 3.30   b 4.30

LISTENING 3 Listen to Liu Xiaochun talking about his school. Copy and complete the card in English.

Student Card

Name: *Liu Xiaochun*
Nationality:
Country where studying:
Number of students in class:
School starts:
School finishes:

在 zài in

60 六十

Chapter 4 学校

4 Read the texts about three students from different schools. Copy and complete the table in English.

1. 我叫小英,我十三岁。我们班有十四个男学生,十二个女学生。我们八点半上学,四点十分放学。我喜欢历史课和科学课。

2. 我叫小明,我十二岁。我的学校在英国。我的学校有男学生,没有女学生。我们班有十七个学生。我八点上学,三点半放学。我喜欢中文课,也喜欢数学课。

3. 我叫王欢,我十四岁。我们学校有女学生,没有男学生。我的班有十九个学生。我七点四十五分上学,五点二十分放学。我喜欢德文课和地理课。

Grammar

The uses of 在 zài

在 zài can be used in two different ways:
- as a verb. 在 zài means 'to be located'.
- as a preposition. Here 在 means 'in', 'on' or 'at'. The sentence structure for 在 as a preposition is: subject + 在 + place + verb. For example:

姐姐在北京学习。 jiě jie zài běi jīng xué xí
My older sister is studying in Beijing. (literally 'My older sister in Beijing is studying').

我在家上网。 wǒ zài jiā shàng wǎng. I surf the Internet at home.

Name	Age	Number of male students	Number of female students	School starts at	School finishes at	Lessons they like

5 Practise writing the following key characters for this unit. Remember: finish what is inside the box before you close it.

国　男　女

6 Fill in the gaps to complete a paragraph about your school life. Use Activity 4 to help you.

我 (name),我是 (nationality)。我们班有 〔👦〕 和 〔👧〕。

我喜欢 (subject) 课和 (subject) 课。我 (time) 上学,(time) 放学。

7 In pairs, ask and answer the questions about school.

1. 你们班有多少学生？ nǐ men bān yǒu duō shǎo xué sheng

2. 你们班有多少中国/英国学生？ nǐ men bān yǒu duō shǎo zhōng guó/yīng guó xué sheng

3. 你们班有多少男学生/女学生？ nǐ men bān yǒu duō shǎo nán xué sheng/nǚ xué sheng

4. 你几点上学/放学？ nǐ jǐ diǎn shàng xué/fàng xué

⑤ 中国的学校 zhōng guó de xué xiào   Schools in China

Discovering schools in China

学生数 Number of students in China in 2007

普通本专科 Undergraduates in universities and colleges	18,848,954 [1]
普通高中 Students in senior high school	25,224,008
普通初中 Students in junior high school	57,208,992 [2]
普通小学 Children in primary school	105,640,027 [3]
学前教育 Children in pre-school/nursery	23,488,300

From the website: http://www.moe.edu.cn/, Ministry of Education of the People's Republic of China

[1] The total population of Australia is 21 million.
[2] The total population of the UK is 61 million.
[3] This is the same as the population of Spain and France added together.

中国的教育 zhōng guó de jiào yù Education in China

Chinese parents feel that giving their children a good education is extremely important. Most Chinese children work hard in school, and young people sometimes feel pressure from their parents' expectations, especially if they are the only child in the family: the parents and both sets of grandparents have only one child's achievements to focus on.

Compulsory education in China lasts nine years: primary school (six years) and junior high school (three years). Students then decide whether to stay on for senior high school (three years); after that, they may go to vocational school or university.

The school year has two terms, with long summer and winter holidays (during Chinese New Year/Spring Festival) and shorter holidays for International Labour Day (1 May), National Day (1 October), International Children's Day (1 June) for primary pupils, as well as some traditional festivals.

小学 xiǎo xué Primary school

Children start school at the age of six. The school day is much longer than in the UK. It can start as early as 7.30am and carry on until 4 or 5pm. Classes usually have around 40 to 50 students. The core subjects include Chinese, mathematics, English, P.E., art and music. At some schools other subjects including science and craft may also be offered. Even at primary school, there is a lot of homework.

The class generally has the same teacher for all subjects, and pupils are given various positions such as class president and subject representatives, as well as individual responsibility for classroom decoration, tidiness and recreation. Breaktime is lots of fun, with some traditional Chinese games such as kicking the shuttlecock and skipping and other group activities. To keep fit, students do group exercises at school every morning. Children also enjoy school trips to museums, parks and zoos.

Chapter 4 学校

中学 zhōng xué Secondary school

Secondary school consists of junior high school (初中 chū zhōng, 3 years) and senior high school (高中 gāo zhōng, 3 years), preparing pupils for university entry exams (高考 gāo kǎo) at the end of the six years. Subjects range from Chinese, maths, English, history, geography, politics and the sciences to music, art and P.E. In the second year of senior high school, students are divided into humanities and sciences classes to specialise in either one. However, Chinese, maths and English are still compulsory for everybody. The school day does not finish until the evening.

Many secondary school students must do military training (军训 jūn xùn) for a week or two each year. Its main purpose is to build up physical strength and to teach students to live in a harsher environment than their day-to-day life. As in primary schools, students develop a strong connection with their class because school days are long and the same group stays together for most classes.

Students have to work particularly hard for the entrance exams to senior high school and then university (大学 dà xué). Only about 18 percent of Chinese students go to university, so competition for places is fierce.

LISTENING 1 Listen to three people introducing themselves. Fill in the table with Chinese characters or English.

Name	Type of school	Subjects he/she likes

READING 2 Do some research on schools in China on the Internet or using other resources. Choose either a primary school or secondary school. Use the following questions to help you prepare a short presentation.

- How many terms are there in a school?
- How many students are there in a school and a class?
- How many subjects do students learn?
- How many lessons do students have a week?
- What time do students go to school and finish classes?
- How long do students spend on homework every day?

六十三 63

汉字 hàn zì Investigating characters

Learning more about Chinese characters

Often one part of a Chinese character gives a hint about the meaning (the radical), while another part gives a hint about the pronunciation. This can sometimes help you guess how to pronounce an unfamiliar character and give you a clue to the general area of meaning, although your guess may not always be correct.

READING 1

The characters below contain the same part, 青 (qīng), which tells you the pronunciation of the characters. Match each of the English meanings with the correct Chinese character, using the radicals to help you.

Meanings of the radicals: 1 氵 water; 2 日 sun, day; 3 忄 heart; 4 讠 speech

1 清 qīng   a sunny
2 晴 qíng   b to ask, to invite
3 情 qíng   c clear (liquid)
4 请 qǐng   d feeling, love

部首 bù shǒu Radicals

To understand Chinese characters, it helps to learn the meanings of their radicals, especially the most common ones.

讠

The radical 讠 comes from the character 言 (yán, 'word/speak'). Characters that have 讠 as the radical are usually related to languages or speaking. For example, 说 (shuō, 'speak/talk'), 话 (huà, 'saying/word'), 课 (kè, 'class/lesson').

囗

The radical 囗 is different from 口. When 囗 is a radical, it represents a border or an enclosed area. For example:

国 guó country   园 yuán park   囚 qiú prisoner

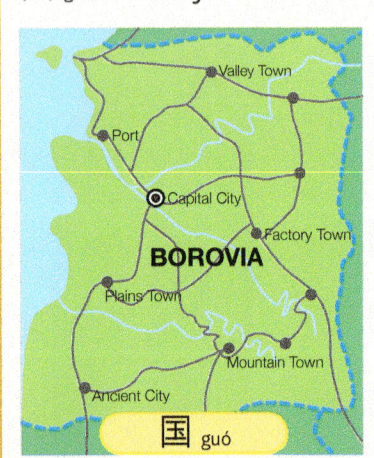

国 guó   园 yuán   囚 qiú

64 六十四

Chapter 4 学校

READING 2 Look at the radicals below. Then group the list of characters (a-x) according to radical.

Example: **1** d, l, p

1 亻 person	2 力 strength	3 土 earth	4 子 child
5 犭 animal	6 辶 to go	7 火 fire	8 木 wood

a 树 (tree)　　　　b 地 (land)　　　　c 这 (this)　　　　d 做 (to do)

e 努 (to exert)　　f 场 (field)　　　　g 动 (to move/act)　h 林 (forest)

i 猪 (pig)　　　　j 孙 (grandson)　　k 本 (root)　　　　l 他 (he)

m 进 (move forward)　n 狗 (dog)　　　o 炒 (to stir-fry)　p 你 (you)

q 烧 (to burn)　　r 猫 (cat)　　　　s 边 (edge/side)　　t 灯 (lamp)

u 学 (to learn)　　v 孩 (child)　　　w 尘 (dust)　　　　x 男 (male)

WRITING 3 Your new Chinese penpal 牛天 Niu Tian has emailed you with some questions for you to answer. You don't need to use full sentences.

Example: **1** 十三岁

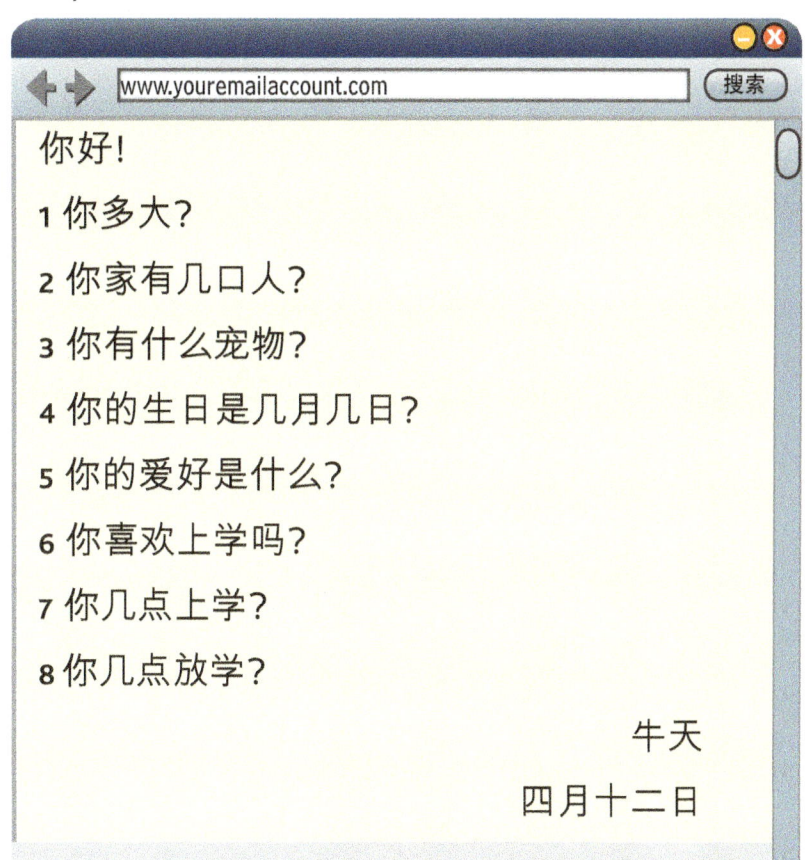

---

www.youremailaccount.com　　搜索

你好！

1 你多大？

2 你家有几口人？

3 你有什么宠物？

4 你的生日是几月几日？

5 你的爱好是什么？

6 你喜欢上学吗？

7 你几点上学？

8 你几点放学？

牛天

四月十二日

Extension

LISTENING 1 Liu Yan is Dawei's new friend. Listen to their conversation and answer the questions in English.

1. How many lessons does Liu Yan have today?
2. List two lessons she has in the morning.
3. Which two lessons does she have in the afternoon?
4. What lessons does she like?
5. When does she have a Chinese lesson?
6. How many male and female students are there in her class?

Liu Yan

Dawei

SPEAKING 2 Work in pairs. You are new to a school and have a lot of questions about your partner and the school. Use the examples below to ask and answer each other's questions.

A: 你几点上学？

B: 我 (time) 上学。

A: 你几点放学？

B: 我 (time) 放学。

A: 你学什么？

B: 我学 (subject 1)、(subject 2) 和 (subject 3)。

A: 你会说 (language) 吗？

B: 我会说/不会说 (language)。

A: 你喜欢什么课？

B: 我喜欢 (subjects)。

A: 你星期几有 (subject) 课？

B: 我 (day of the week) 有 (subject) 课。

A: 你几点上 (subject) 课？

B: 我 (time) 上 (subject)。

A: 你们班有多少 (students/male/female students)？

B: 我们班有 (number of students/male/female students)。

说 shuō to talk, speak

READING 3 Read the text and decide which of the statements below are true.

Micah 是英国人，十五岁。他的班有十三个女学生，八个男学生。有五个德国学生、七个法国学生、九个英国学生。他们上午有中文课，下午学数学、科学和中国历史。他们八点十分上课，四点五十放学。

Micah 会说中文，也会说法文，他喜欢上网学中文。他也喜欢运动，星期六他和爸爸打网球，星期天他和弟弟玩儿滑板。

1 Micah is Chinese.

2 He is a teenager.

3 There are more male students than female in his class.

4 The students are from China, Britain and Germany.

5 There are fewer students from Germany than elsewhere.

6 They learn Chinese in the morning.

7 They also learn Chinese history.

8 They finish school at 5.40pm.

9 Micah can also speak French.

10 He plays tennis on Sunday.

WRITING 4 Fill in the gaps according to the English or pictures.

1 (I am) ____ 。 (I like learning) ____ 。

2 我们班 (has 10 male students)，(8 female students)。

3 我 (at 11.20am on Mondays) 有数学课。

WRITING 5 Use Activity 4 to help you write about yourself.

Review

I can:

1
- list school subjects — 中文 zhōng wén, 英文 yīng wén, 法文 fǎ wén, 德文 dé wén, 科学 kē xué, 数学 shù xué, 历史 lì shǐ, 地理 dì lǐ, 体育 tǐ yù, 音乐 yīn yuè
- ask what subjects people like — 你喜欢什么课？
- say what I study on different days — 我星期三有历史课。
- use question word 什么 shén me — 这是什么书？
- write new characters — 中、文、学、英、课

2
- tell the time — 上午十点二十分 shàng wǔ shí diǎn èr shí fēn / 下午一点半 xià wǔ yī diǎn bàn
- say what time I have lessons — 我上午十点有体育课。
- use the question word 几 jǐ — 你几点有地理课？
- understand the order of time words — 我星期一上午十点有体育课。
- write new characters — 上、下、午、点、分

3
- use plural pronouns — 我们 wǒ men, 他们 tā men
- use the verb 是 shì 'to be' — 我是老师，他是老师，我们是老师。
- write new characters — 我、你、们

4
- talk about school in more detail — 你几点上学？几点放学？
- use the question word 多少 duō shǎo — 你们班有多少学生？
- use the preposition 在 zài — 我在家上网。
- write new characters — 国、男、女

Investigating characters
- know the difference between the radicals 囗 and 口 — 国、吃
- know about the radical 讠 — 课

68 六十八

Test

Chapter 4 学校

LISTENING 1 Listen to the dialogue between a girl called Xiaoyun and a boy called Zhang Long. True or false? (1–5)

1. Zhang Long likes maths but Xiaoyun does not.
2. Xiaoyun's English lesson is at 2pm.
3. Zhang Long's English lesson is on Thursday afternoon.
4. Zhang Long goes to school at 9.00am.
5. Xiaoyun finishes school at 4pm.
6. Xiaoyun's class is bigger than Zhang Long's class.
7. Xiaoyun likes her Chinese teacher and her geography teacher.
8. Zhang Long doesn't have any geography lessons.

SPEAKING 2 Role play. Ask and answer the questions in Chinese with your partner.

1. 你是 (nationality) 吗？
2. 你学什么 (subject)？
3. 你几点上学？几点放学？
4. 你星期几有中文课？你几点上中文课？
5. 你们班有多少学生？多少男学生？多少女学生？

READING 3 Read Yang Jingjing's school timetable and answer the questions in English.

Yang Jingjing's timetable

		星期一	星期二	星期三	星期四	星期五
上午	8:10	数学	中文	数学	英文	英文
	9:00	英文	数学	中文	中文	数学
	10:10		历史	科学	地理	
	11:00	中文	英文	英文	数学	中文
下午	2:15	美术	政治	体育		体育
	3:15	科学	电脑	数学	历史	政治
	4:20	地理			法文	音乐

1. What time is Yang Jingjing's English lesson on Monday?
2. What lesson does she have at 3.15pm on Wednesday?
3. Which day does she have geography at 10.10am?
4. How many PE lessons does she have in a week?
5. What is her last lesson on Friday?

WRITING 4 Write to your penpal telling him/her about your school. You could include:

- What time do you go to school and what time do you finish classes (放学)?
- How many male students and female students are there in your class (班)?
- What lessons (课) do you like?
- On which day and what time do you have Chinese lessons?

六十九 69

Key language

School subjects

中文	zhōng wén	Chinese	地理	dì lǐ	geography
英文	yīng wén	English	体育	tǐ yù	PE
法文	fǎ wén	French	音乐	yīn yuè	music
德文	dé wén	German	学校	xué xiào	school
科学	kē xué	science	课	kè	lesson
数学	shù xué	maths	学	xué	to learn
历史	lì shǐ	history			

Time

几点？	jǐ diǎn	What time?	分	fēn	minute
点	diǎn	o'clock	上午	shàng wǔ	morning
半	bàn	half	下午	xià wǔ	afternoon

School

你们	nǐ men	you (plural)	学生	xué sheng	student
我们	wǒ men	we	男学生	nán xué sheng	male student
上学	shàng xué	to go to school	女学生	nǚ xué sheng	female student
放学	fàng xué	to finish classes	中国	zhōng guó	China
吃	chī	to eat	英国	yīng guó	Britain
午饭	wǔ fàn	lunch	多少	duō shǎo	how many/how much
班	bān	class	节	jié	a measure word for lessons

Stroke order

中	中 丨 口 中
文	文 丶 亠 文
学	学 学 学 学 学 学 学 学
英	英 一 艹 英 英 英 英 英 英
课	课 课 课 课 课 课 课 课 课
上	丨 上 上
下	一 丁 下
午	丿 午 午 午
点	丨 卜 占 占 占 占 点 点
分	八 八 分 分
我	我 二 千 手 我 我 我
你	你 亻 亻 你 你 你 你
们	丿 亻 亻 们 们
国	囗 冂 冂 冃 用 国 国 国
男	男 男 男 田 田 男 男
女	く 女 女

5 食品和饮料 shí pǐn hé yǐn liào **Food and drink**

1 我吃米饭 wǒ chī mǐ fàn *I eat rice*

❀ Talking about what you like to eat and drink

LISTENING 1 Listen to Li Mengfei going through her shopping list and write down the letters of the pictures you hear her mention. (1–9)

www.jinbufood.cn 搜索

超市.cn

搜索 Search　价格 Price　下一个 Next Item　购买 Buy　付账 Pay

- a 面包 miàn bāo
- b 鸡蛋 jī dàn
- c 面条 miàn tiáo
- d 米饭 mǐ fàn
- e 比萨饼 bǐ sà bǐng
- f 水 shuǐ
- g 茶 chá
- h 水果 shuǐ guǒ
- i 果汁 guǒ zhī

READING 2 Match the shopping list with the correct basket.

1. 面包、鸡蛋、米饭、水、果汁
2. 水、面条、面包、茶、果汁
3. 面包、鸡蛋、面条、米饭、比萨饼
4. 鸡蛋、比萨饼、水、茶、果汁

a　b　c 面条　d 面条

72 七十二

Chapter 5 食品和饮料

SPEAKING 3 In pairs: one person reads out one of the shopping lists from Activity 2 and the other finds the correct one. Then swap.

LISTENING 4 Listen to these people talking about themselves and their likes and dislikes. Copy and complete the grid with the letters of the correct pictures from Activity 1. (1–4)

Name	👍	👎
Xiaoli	d	b

吃 chī to eat
喝 hē to drink

Grammar

Like/dislike with food and drink

In English we usually say 'I like pizza', 'I like coffee'. In Chinese, you usually add the verbs for eating/drinking when saying what you like or dislike:

我喜欢吃/喝… wǒ xǐ huan chī/hē… 'I like eating/drinking…'
我不喜欢吃/喝… wǒ bù xǐ huan chī/hē… 'I don't like eating/drinking…'

SPEAKING 5 In pairs, talk about what you like/dislike to eat or drink.

我喜欢吃 / 喝 … wǒ xǐ huan chī / hē …
我不喜欢吃 / 喝 … wǒ bù xǐ huan chī / hē …

LISTENING 6 Listen to Li An talking about his family and answer the questions in English.

1. How many people are there in the family?
2. When is Dad's birthday?
3. What does Dad like to eat and drink?
4. Whose birthday is on 9 June?
5. What does Li An like to eat and drink? What does he dislike?
6. Who else likes pizza apart from Li An?

WRITING 7 Practise writing the following key characters for this unit. For more help with stroke order, look at page 89.

米　饭　水　果　汁

WRITING 8 Put together the characters from Activity 7 to make the following words.

1. fruit
2. fruit juice
3. rice

七十三　73

② 你午饭吃什么？ nǐ wǔ fàn chī shén me — What do you have for lunch?

🌸 Talking about different kinds of food and drink

READING 1 Read the meal plan for these two families and answer the questions.

小月家：

星期一	星期二	星期三	星期四	星期五	星期六	星期日
米饭	面条	比萨饼	炒面	包子	米饭	饺子

Jamel 家：

星期一	星期二	星期三	星期四	星期五	星期六	星期日
比萨饼	面条	炒面	比萨饼	面包	炒饭	炒面

1. What does Xiaoyue's family have on Tuesday?
2. What does Jamel's family have on Saturday?
3. On which days does Xiaoyue's family have rice?
4. On which days does Jamel's family have pizza?

饺子

包子

| 炒面 | chǎo miàn | fried noodles | 饺子 | jiǎo zi | Chinese dumplings |
| 炒饭 | chǎo fàn | fried rice | 包子 | bāo zi | steamed stuffed bun |

LISTENING 2 Listen to the conversation between Caitlin and Ke Feifei. True or false?

1. Ke Feifei likes noodles.
2. Caitlin likes Chinese dumplings.
3. Caitlin's mum and dad like fried rice.
4. Caitlin's mum likes Chinese tea.
5. Ke Feifei's dad likes pizza.
6. Ke Feifei's mum like pizza too.
7. Ke Feifei's mum likes rice and noodles.

74　七十四

Chapter 5 食品和饮料

SPEAKING 3 In pairs, talk about what you and your family like/dislike to eat and drink. You can use the sample dialogue to help you.

咖啡 kā fēi coffee

A: 你喜欢吃米饭吗？ nǐ xǐ huan chī mǐ fàn ma

B: 不喜欢，我喜欢吃炒面。 bù xǐ huan, wǒ xǐ huan chī chǎo miàn
我喜欢喝咖啡，你呢？ wǒ xǐ huan hē kā fēi, nǐ ne

A: 我也喜欢喝咖啡,我爸爸妈妈喜欢喝中国茶，你爸爸妈妈喜欢喝茶吗？ wǒ yě xǐ huan hē kā fēi, wǒ bà ba mā ma xǐ huan hē zhōng guó chá, nǐ bà ba mā ma xǐ huan hē chá ma

B: 喜欢，他们喜欢喝茶，他们喜欢中国茶，也喜欢英国茶。 xǐ huan, tā men xǐ huan hē chá, tā men xǐ huan zhōng guó chá, yě xǐ huan yīng guó chá

Culture

中国茶 zhōng gúo chá **Chinese tea**

Tea is an important part of Chinese culture. The book 茶经 (chá jīng, the Tea Classic) was written between 760 and 780 – more than 1200 years ago! – so tea in China has a long history and many people are very knowledgeable about it. The best tea costs more than the finest wines.

Chinese people drink tea every day. This could be 绿茶 (lǜ chá, 'green tea'), 红茶 (hóng chá, literally 'red tea' but meaning black tea) or 花茶 (huā chá, 'flower tea' – usually jasmine.) People tend to drink more black tea in cold weather for its warming properties and green tea in hot weather for its cooling properties – but most Chinese people prefer to drink their tea hot, not iced, even in the summer.

WRITING 4 Practise writing the following key characters for this unit. For more help with stroke order, look at page 89.

| 吃 | 喝 | 炒 | 他 | 她 |

WRITING 5 Label the food in Chinese.

1   2   3   4   5

WRITING 6 Write your own meal plan for a week, using the characters you've learnt to write so far.

Example: 星期一：米饭

七十五 75

3 一日三餐 yí rì sān cān Daily meals

🌸 Talking about mealtimes

LISTENING 1 You are new at school and Waleed is telling you the canteen menu for the week. Write down the days of the week in Chinese, then listen and note in English the food eaten on each day.

Example: 星期一 rice, beef and chicken

noodles	fried rice	fried noodles
beef		chicken
pork	rice	fish	lamb
fried eggs		pizza

牛奶	niú nǎi	milk
牛肉	niú ròu	beef
猪肉	zhū ròu	pork
羊肉	yáng ròu	lamb
鸡肉	jī ròu	chicken

LISTENING 2 Listen to and read the Chinese sentences, then choose the correct option from the English sentences. (1–6)

Example: **1 a**

早饭	zǎo fàn	breakfast
午饭	wǔ fàn	lunch
晚饭	wǎn fàn	dinner

1	我们早饭吃面包。	We have (**a** bread **b** eggs) for breakfast.
2	他们午饭吃炒饭。	They have fried rice for (**a** lunch **b** dinner).
3	哥哥晚饭吃比萨饼，喝咖啡。	Older brother has pizza and (**a** coffee **b** tea) for dinner.
4	妈妈晚饭吃饺子，喝茶。她喜欢喝茶。	Mum has dumplings and tea for (**a** lunch **b** dinner).
5	弟弟早上不吃饭。	Younger brother does not eat (**a** breakfast **b** lunch).
6	爸爸早饭吃面条，喝英国茶。	Dad has (**a** bread **b** noodles) and English tea for breakfast.

Grammar

Word order

When you say what you have for breakfast, lunch, etc. you put the words in the following order:
subject (I, you, Mum, etc.) + *meal* (breakfast, etc.) + *verb* + *food* (noodles, etc.).
我午饭吃炒面。 'I lunch eat fried noodles.' = I have fried noodles for lunch.

Pinyin

Pronouncing 'zhi' and 'zhu'

Listen and repeat the sounds in four tones:
zhī/zhū, zhí/zhú, zhǐ/zhǔ, zhì/zhù.
Now listen and repeat these sentences:
蜘蛛织网 zhī zhū zhī wǎng Spider makes web.
蜘蛛喝果汁 zhī zhū hē guǒ zhī Spider drinks fruit juice.

76 七十六

Chapter 5 食品和饮料

WRITING 3 Practise writing the following key characters for this unit.
Then put together characters you've learnt so far in this chapter to make as many words/phrases as possible. There are at least five!

牛 肉 面

Example: 牛 + 肉 = 牛肉 beef

SPEAKING 4 In pairs, take it in turns to say who eats what for different meals.

Example: 她早饭吃鸡蛋。 tā zǎo fàn chī jī dàn

早饭　　午饭　　晚饭

1 她　　2 我们　　3 你　　4 他们

WRITING 5 Choose a person from Activity 4 and write what they eat and drink for breakfast or lunch, using the characters you've learnt.

Example: 她吃炒饭，喝果汁。

READING 6 True or false? Write the correct answer if it is false.

Example: **1** True

1 You can have bread and coffee for breakfast.
2 You can have fried noodles for breakfast.
3 Lunch is between 11 am and 3.00 pm.
4 Dumplings are served between 5 and 11 pm.
5 Both lamb and chicken are served in the evenings.

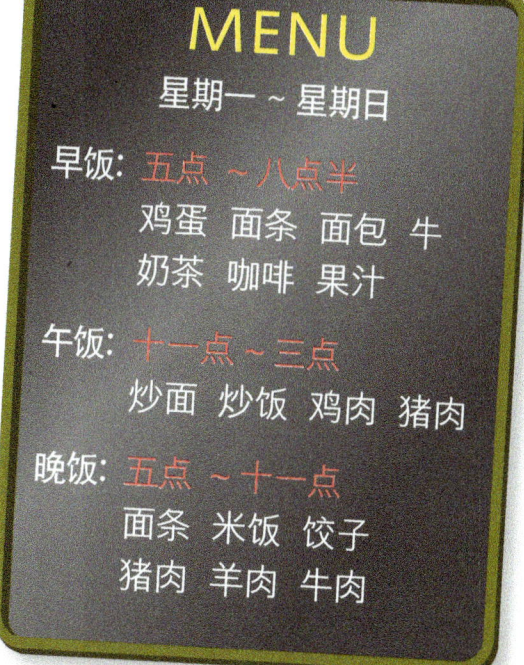

MENU

星期一 ~ 星期日

早饭： 五点 ~ 八点半
鸡蛋　面条　面包　牛
奶茶　咖啡　果汁

午饭： 十一点 ~ 三点
炒面　炒饭　鸡肉　猪肉

晚饭： 五点 ~ 十一点
面条　米饭　饺子
猪肉　羊肉　牛肉

七十七　77

④ 我想喝可乐 wǒ xiǎng hē kě lè I would like a coke

🌸 Ordering in a restaurant

LISTENING 1 Listen to four short conversations between a waiter and customers who are ordering food. Note down the letter of the correct pictures. (1–4)

Example: **1 d, e, a**

a b c d
e f g h

Pinyin

Pronouncing 'c'

In Chinese, 'c' sounds like a tz or a ts. Say the word 'cats', then just say 'ts'. Listen and repeat 'c' and 'cai' in four tones: c, cāi, cái, cǎi, cài.

Now listen and repeat the following:

擦桌子。 cā zhuō zi Wipe the table.

兔子吃草和菜。 tù zi chī cǎo hé cài Rabbits eat grass and vegetables.

饭馆 fàn guǎn restaurant

菜 cài vegetable

炒 chǎo to stir fry

SPEAKING 2 Pair work. Pretend you are in a restaurant and one person (A) is the waiter/waitress and the other (B) is the customer. A asks B what he/she wants and B replies with his/her order. Use the grammar box to help you.

Grammar

The use of 想 xiǎng

想 xiǎng is often used to mean 'want to/would like to' and is usually followed by another verb.

我想吃… wǒ xiǎng chī = I would like to eat…

我想喝… wǒ xiǎng hē = I would like to drink…

78 七十八

Chapter 5 食品和饮料

LISTENING 3 A boy called Li Wen and a girl called Zhang Tianying are eating in a local restaurant. Listen to their conversation and answer the questions.

张天英   李文

1 What would Li Wen like to eat?
2 What would Zhang Tianying like to eat?
3 What would Zhang Tianying like to drink?
4 What would Li Wen like to drink?
5 What did both of them want to have at the end?

碗 wǎn bowl (also a measure word)   冰淇淋 bīng qí lín ice cream
杯 bēi cup/glass (also a measure word)   巧克力 qiǎo kè lì chocolate

SPEAKING 4 Work in groups of three or four. You are eating out with your friend. One person is the waiter/waitress and the others are customers. Use these phrases to help you.

Waiter/waitress:
你们想吃/喝什么？ nǐ men xiǎng chī/hē shén me
我们有… wǒ men yǒu
我们没有… wǒ men méi yǒu

Customer:
你们有…吗？ nǐ men yǒu…ma
我想吃/喝… wǒ xiǎng chī/hē
我喜欢吃/喝… wǒ xǐ huan chī/hē

WRITING 5 Practise writing the following key characters for this unit. For more help with stroke order, look at page 89.

茶   菜   想

WRITING 6 Complete the letter from Olivia with the Chinese for the pictures.

你好！
　　我叫 Olivia。
　　我家有四口人，爸爸、妈妈、我和弟弟。妈妈三十八岁，爸爸四十岁，我十二岁，弟弟九岁。我 1 🍳 吃鸡蛋，喝 2 🥛 。我妈妈 3 👍 吃面条、4 🍚 和 5 🥗 。爸爸和弟弟 6 🧳 吃 7 🍖 ，爸爸 8 👍 喝 9 🍵 。

Olivia
十月九日

七十九 79

⑤ 中国菜 zhōng guó cài **Chinese food**

❀ Regional food

Chinese food eaten abroad does not reflect the many different styles of food eaten in China. Generally, people in northern China prefer using flour/wheat, for example in noodles and steamed bread, while people in southern China eat more rice. Sichuan in the west of China is famous for its hot and spicy food, and Shanghai is well-known for its sweet and sour dishes.

READING 1 Match the names of the dishes below with their pictures on the map, using the characters and radicals you have learned to help you.

1 北京烤鸭   2 甜酸鱼   3 拉面   4 香港小吃

80 八十

Eating habits and chopsticks (筷子 kuài zi)

At home or in a restaurant, every person has their own bowl (with rice or noodles) in front of them. In the middle of the table there are plates of meat and vegetable dishes to be shared. In restaurants, for a big group, there is sometimes a rotating surface on a round table (a lazy susan).

Chinese people use chopsticks to eat with. These may be made from bamboo, wood, plastic, porcelain or metal. There is a 'right' and a 'wrong' way to use chopsticks. You should pick your food up instead of 'stabbing' it with a chopstick. It is also considered very rude to point at someone with your chopsticks, or to play with them at the table, or tap on your glass or plate with them.

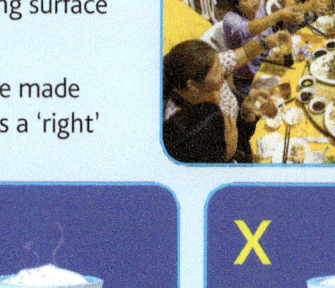

READING 2 In groups, discuss what you think might be the reason why resting chopsticks upright is wrong.

Eating out

There are many different types of restaurants in Chinese cities. Apart from traditional ones doing regional food (such as 四川 sì chuān, 湖南 hú nán, 江西 jiāng xī), you can find restaurants specialising in seafood, hot pot, noodles, vegetarian food, soup or even porridge! Fast-food restaurants including McDonald's 麦当劳 mài dāng láo and KFC 肯德鸡 kěn dé jī can be found nowadays in many cities.

Chinese people love to go out to eat with family, friends or colleagues. You can choose anything from the food stalls on the street to a private dining room in a restaurant.

Chinese breakfast

Chinese breakfast is very different from what we have here. Instead of cereal or toast, people eat things like dumpling soup 馄饨 hún tun, pan-fried dumplings 锅贴 guō tiē, steamed twisted rolls 花卷 huā juǎn, jellied bean curd 豆腐脑儿 dòu fu nǎor, 'Eight Treasure' rice porridge 八宝粥 bā bǎo zhōu and deep-fried twisted dough sticks 油条 yóu tiáo. In some areas, like Guangdong 广东 guǎng dōng in southern China, people sometimes go to a restaurant for a dim sum breakfast 早茶 zǎo chá which can last for hours!

汉字 hàn zì Investigating characters

Learning more about Chinese characters

READING 1
Look at the radicals and characters. Discuss in groups why these characters have the radicals.

火 is both a character and a radical meaning 'fire'.
炒 = to stir fry   烟 = smoke
灾 = disaster

饣 is a radical meaning 'food' or 'meal'.
饭 = food/meal   饭馆 = restaurant
饼 = a round flat cake/pie/pastry
饿 = hungry

艹 is a radical meaning 'grass' or 'plant'.
茶 = tea   菜 = vegetable
草 = grass   药 = medicine

READING 2
Find the radicals in the following characters. Then match the characters to their English meaning with the help of the radicals.

Example: **1 b**

1 花	a hungry	5 灰	a hungry
2 烧	b flower	6 饥	b ash
3 饿	c to burn	7 葡萄	c lake
4 喊	d to shout	8 湖	d grapes

9 妻	a medicine	13 狼	a language
10 说	b coal	14 炉	b stove
11 煤	c to talk/speak	15 囚	c wolf
12 药	d wife	16 语	d prisoner

82 八十二

Chapter 5 食品和饮料

READING 3

Work in groups and read the following passages. You won't know every character, but try to work out the general meaning. You may be able to guess something of the meaning of the characters from the radicals.

1. 我们家星期天去了饭馆吃饭,我们很饿,我们吃了米饭、肉和菜。我们喝了葡萄汁和中国茶。爸爸说:"今天的饭很好吃!"

2. 他家的花园很大,花园里有很多花、草和蔬菜,花园里也有葡萄、草莓和苹果。

WRITING 4

Write one or two characters and their English meanings for each of these radicals.

Example: 口: 喝 to drink

女   火
氵   口
讠   艹
忄

WRITING 5

Poppy is trying to write about her pet dog in Chinese, but she has forgotten some of the characters. You need to help her fill the gap by choosing and writing the correct words.

四　大　喝　吃　球　叫

我有一只 __1__ 狗 __2__ Flick。他 __3__ 岁。他喜欢 __4__ 肉,他也喜欢 __5__ 果汁。他很喜欢玩儿 __6__ 。

Language

How many Chinese characters do you need to learn?

There are over 80,000 Chinese characters, but most of them are rarely used. Most printed texts use a much smaller group of commonly used characters.
- The most frequently used **1,000** characters make up **90%** of all texts;
- The most frequently used **2,500** characters: **98%**;
- The most frequently used **3,500** characters: **99.5%**.

This proves that in order to understand everyday Chinese, you don't need to learn huge numbers of Chinese characters.

Extension

1 Patrick is in a school summer camp in China. A journalist has interviewed him to find out more about young people from a different culture. Answer the questions.

1. How old is Patrick?
2. What did Patrick say about his pet snake?
3. What is Patrick's favourite school subject and why?
4. What is Patrick's favourite food?
5. What did Patrick say about Chinese food?
6. What do Patrick's mum and dad like?
7. What was the journalist's last question?
8. What did Patrick say in response to the final question?

2 You are making a short audio clip to introduce yourself to your Chinese friend. You can choose any three or all of the following parts.

Basics about yourself: name, age, birthday

我叫 __ 。

我 __ 岁。

我的生日是 __ 。

Your family and pet

我家有 __ 口人。

我有 __ (爸爸、妈妈…)。

我有一只 / 条 __ 。

Your hobbies

我喜欢打 / 踢 / 玩儿 / 看 __ 。

School: subjects you like/dislike, when you have lessons, your class

我喜欢 __ 课。

我不喜欢 __ 课。

我星期 __ 有 __ 课。

我们班有 __ 个 男学生 / __ 女学生。

Food you like/dislike

我喜欢吃/喝 __ 。

84 八十四

Chapter 5 食品和饮料

READING 3 Read the messages on the website and answer the questions.

Name	Birthday	Hobbies	Food like	Food dislike	Pet
 方林	四月七日	上网	面包	水果	一只狗
 月天	十月六日	打网球 打乒乓球	面条	鸡蛋	两条鱼
 大中	十二月三十日	看书	比萨饼	米饭	一只鸟
 小欢	五月十八日	看电视	水果	比萨饼	一只猫

1 Whose birthday is 6 October?
2 Who likes going online?
3 Whose favourite food is pizza?
4 Who doesn't like fruit?
5 Whose hobby is watching TV?
6 Who doesn't like rice?
7 Who likes noodles and dislikes eggs?
8 Who has a bird?

READING 4 Read Dazhong's birthday plans and answer the questions.

要 yào to want

1 What date is Dazhong's birthday?
2 What does he want for his birthday?
3 What are his plans for the morning?
4 What are his plans for the afternoon?

十二月三十日(星期六)是我的生日！
我要一个篮球和一个滑板，我喜欢运动！
上午：踢足球、看电视、吃比萨饼
下午：看电影、买东西、吃生日面条

WRITING 5 Write what each person likes and dislikes in Chinese sentences.

1 Danny
2 Angelina 
3 Meihua 
4 Xiaoping 

八十五 85

Review

I can:

1
- list food and drink — 面包 miàn bāo, 鸡蛋 jī dàn, 水果 shuǐ guǒ, 米饭 mǐ fàn, 果汁 guǒ zhī, 茶 chá
- use verbs 喜欢 and 吃/喝 to say what food/drink I like/dislike — 我喜欢吃面包。他不喜欢喝水。
- write new food/drink characters — 米、饭、水、果、汁

2
- say and understand more food/drink words — 炒饭 chǎo fàn, 炒面 chǎo miàn, 饺子 jiǎo zi, 包子 bāo zi
- say what I and other people eat on different days — 我星期一吃炒饭。 wǒ xīng qī yī chī chǎo fàn
他们星期日吃饺子。 tā men xīng qī rì chī jiǎo zi
- write new characters — 吃、喝、炒、他、她

3
- talk about what I eat and drink for different meals — 我早饭吃面包，喝牛奶。 wǒ zǎo fàn chī miàn bāo hē niú nǎi
- use the correct word order when talking about mealtimes — 她星期六晚饭吃包子。 tā xīng qī liù wǎn fàn chī bāo zi
- read a menu — 米饭、羊肉面条、鸡肉炒面、鸡蛋炒饭、饺子、包子、炒牛肉、猪肉、茶、咖啡、果汁
- write new characters — 肉、牛、面

4
- order food/drink in a restaurant using 想 — 想 吃/喝 xiǎng chī/hē
- use measure words 碗 wǎn, 杯 bēi — 一碗米饭，两杯水
- write new characters — 茶、菜、想

Investigating characters
- recognise radicals — 火、亻、艹

Test

Chapter 5 食品和饮料

LISTENING 1 Listen to a conversation between a customer and the waiter in a restaurant and answer the questions.

1. What did the customer order first?
2. What did the waiter offer the customer?
3. Did the customer accept what he recommended?
4. What drink did she order?

SPEAKING 2 Describe what each person eats and drinks for each meal.

…早饭吃/喝 zǎo fàn chī/hē…

…午饭喝 wǔ fàn chī/hē…

…晚饭吃/喝 wǎn fàn chī/hē…

Mia

Daniel

READING 3 Fang Ji talks about her family's diet. Note down in English what each person likes or dislikes.

1. 我哥哥喜欢吃菜，不喜欢吃肉。
2. 我爸爸喜欢吃米饭、喝茶。他不喜欢喝咖啡。
3. 我和妈妈喜欢吃饺子，也喜欢吃包子。
4. 我的小猫喜欢吃鱼、喝牛奶。

WRITING 4 A few labels are missing. Fill in the gaps.

1 ___   水   2 ___   牛奶   炒面

3 ___   包子   4 ___   菜   5 ___

八十七 87

Key language

Food

面包	miàn bāo	bread	牛肉	niú ròu	beef
面条	miàn tiáo	noodles	羊肉	yáng ròu	lamb/mutton
面	miàn	wheat flour; noodles	猪肉	zhū ròu	pork
米饭	mǐ fàn	(cooked) rice	肉	ròu	meat
炒饭	chǎo fàn	fried rice	鸡肉	jī ròu	chicken (meat)
饭	fàn	meal; cooked rice	鸡蛋	jī dàn	(chicken) egg
炒面	chǎo miàn	fried noodles	菜	cài	vegetable
炒	chǎo	to stir fry	比萨饼	bǐ sà bǐng	pizza
饺子	jiǎo zi	Chinese dumplings (with meat and/or vegetable stuffing)	水果	shuǐ guǒ	fruit
			巧克力	qiǎo kè lì	chocolate
包子	bāo zi	steamed stuffed bun	冰淇淋	bīng qí lín	ice cream

Drinks

水	shuǐ	water	牛奶	niú nǎi	milk
茶	chá	tea	咖啡	kā fēi	coffee
果汁	guǒ zhī	fruit juice			

Daily meals

吃	chī	to eat	杯	bēi	glass/cup (measure word as well)
喝	hē	to drink	碗	wǎn	bowl (measure word as well)
早饭	zǎo fàn	breakfast			
早上	zǎo shang	morning	想	xiǎng	would like to; want to
午饭	wǔ fàn	lunch			
晚饭	wǎn fàn	dinner	饭馆	fàn guǎn	restaurant
晚上	wǎn shang	evening/night			

Stroke order

米	丶	丷	丷	半	米	米					
饭	丿	饣	饣	饣	饣	饭	饭				
水	亅	刀	水	水							
果	丨	口	口	曰	早	甲	果	果			
汁	丶	氵	氵	汁	汁						
吃	丨	口	口	口	吃	吃					
喝	口	口	口	吗	吗	喝	喝	喝	喝	喝	喝
炒	丶	火	火	火	炒	炒	炒	炒			
他	丿	亻	仁	他	他						
她	𡿨	女	女	如	如	她					
牛	丿	𠂉	牛	牛							
肉	丨	冂	内	内	肉	肉					
面	一	一	厂	丙	而	面	面	面			
茶	一	十	艹	艹	艾	茶	茶	茶			
菜	一	艹	艹	艹	艹	艹	菜	苹	苹	菜	
想	一	十	才	木	村	相	相	相	相	想	想	想

1 读和写 dú hé xiě Reading and Writing A

❀ Extra Reading and Writing practice

READING 1 Read the Chinese and decide if the English translation is correct. If incorrect, write the correct translation.

1. 早上好 good morning
2. 老师好 goodbye
3. 二十 12
4. 再见 hello
5. 我三十一岁。 I am 31 years old.
6. 她六十岁。 She is 60 years old.
7. 她九岁。 She is 7 years old.
8. 他叫 Kenyon, 我叫 Alfredo。 My name is Kenyon and his name is Alfredo.

WRITING 2 Rewrite the numbers in the correct order from smallest to largest.

Example: **d** 十四

| a 九十一 | b 八十六 | c 十七 | d 十四 | e 三十四 |
| f 二十 | g 二十九 | h 四十三 | i 二十八 | j 五十 |

WRITING 3 Write the family members' ages in Chinese.

Example: 张大飞：四十二岁

刘玉：(1) 岁

张书雨：(2) 岁

张云天：(3) 岁

李英芳：(4) 岁

张云天, 73   李英芳, 69   张书雨, 14   刘玉, 38   张大飞, 42

90 九十

1 读和写 dú hé xiě Reading and Writing B

❀ Extra Reading and Writing practice

READING 1 Put characters together to make the following words/phrases. Some characters can be used more than once.

Example: 1 c b

| a 五 | b 六 | c 十 | d 岁 | e 好 | f 你 | g 再 | h 早 | i 上 | j 见 | k 忙 | l 不 |

1 sixteen
2 hello
3 good morning
4 goodbye
5 five years old
6 are you busy?

READING 2 Translate the following from Chinese into English.

1 我叫 Jade, 我八岁。

2 我叫 Manpreet, 我十二岁。

3 你好, 我叫 Anya, 我十四岁。

4 早上好! 我叫 Marie, 我十五岁。他叫 Ian, 他十六岁。

WRITING 3 Look at the pictures and complete the dialogues by using the characters from the box.

| 四 | 六 | 八 | 九 | 十 | 早 | 叫 |

1
__1__ 上好 
__2__ 上好

2
我 __3__ Jasmine。 
我 __4__ Ian。
Jasmine   Ian

3
我叫 Larrisa, 我 __5__ 岁。 
我叫 Rodrick, 我 __6__ 岁。
Larrisa 8   Rodrick 6

4
我 __7__ Yangtong, 我 __8__ 岁。
我 __9__ Liu Ming, 我 __10__ 岁。
Yangtong 14   Liu Ming 10

九十一 91

2 读和写 dú hé xiě Reading and Writing A

❀ Extra reading and writing practice

READING 1 Whose birthday is it?

1 Whose birthday is 25 March?
2 Whose birthday is 7 April?
3 Whose birthday is 3 September?
4 Whose birthday is 8 December?
5 Whose birthday is 30 June?
6 Whose birthday is 19 January?

fāng xiǎo hóng
方小红的生日是六月三十日。
Levi 的生日是四月七日。
lǐ dà tiān
李大天的生日是九月三日。
Naomi 的生日是一月十九日。
liú xīn yuè
刘新乐的生日是十二月八日。
zhào lì li
赵丽丽的生日是三月二十五日。

READING 2 Spot the mistake(s) in the sentences according to the pictures. Note down the differences in English.

1 我有四条鱼。

2 他有一条蛇，他没有猫和狗。

3 我叫 Anna，我家有四口人，我有爸爸、妈妈和一个姐姐。我也有一只大狗。

4 我叫 Michael，我家有五口人，我有爸爸、妈妈、一个姐姐、一个妹妹。我家有一只猫、三只鸟。

WRITING 3 Write down the birthdays.

二月 星期日 5 爸爸
一月 星期三 10 李小鱼
六月 星期一 13 张影
七月 星期三 28 王欢
十二月 星期日 20 弟弟

王欢的生日是 _1_ 。
张影的生日是 _2_ 。 
李小鱼的生日是 _3_ 。 
爸爸的生日是 _4_ 。 
弟弟的生日是 _5_ 。

2 读和写 dú hé xiě Reading and Writing B

❀ Extra reading and writing practice

READING 1 Look at the picture and read the sentences. True or false?

1 小月家有五口人。
2 小月有一个姐姐。
3 小月没有哥哥。
4 小月家有一只狗。
5 小月家没有猫。
6 小月家没有鱼和鸟。

READING 2 Rearrange the Chinese in the correct order to translate the English.

Example: **1** b, a, c, d

1 My birthday is 8 February.
   a 生日 b 我的 c 是 d 二月八日

2 My birthday is 13 January.
   a 是 b 生日 c 一月 d 我的 e 十三日

3 Today is 12 October.
   a 十二日 b 今天 c 是 d 十月

4 Her birthday is today.
   a 是 b 她的 c 生日 d 今天

5 My birthday is 8 April.
   a 四 b 日 c 八 d 我 e 生日 f 的 g 是 h 月

WRITING 3 Complete the sentences according to the pictures.

我 _1_ Michael。

他 _2_ 岁。

她 _3_ 一只大狗和两只 _4_ 猫。

今天是我的 _5_ 。

九十三 93

3 读和写 dú hé xiě Reading and Writing A

❀ Extra reading and writing practice

READING 1 Match the pictures to the Chinese words.

Example: 1 c

a	游泳	b	打网球	c	看电影	d	踢足球
e	玩儿电脑游戏	f	听音乐	g	打篮球	h	看电视
i	看书	j	打乒乓球	k	跑步	l	买东西
m	上网	n	玩儿滑板				

READING 2 Find the following activities in the box. Choose the correct characters for the English.

Example: a: 9, 18, 6

a watch films
b skateboarding
c play computer games
d read books
e go shopping
f listen to music
g surf the Internet
h watch TV

1 视	2 听	3 音	4 乐
5 儿	6 影	7 买	8 东
9 看	10 板	11 网	12 西
13 书	14 滑	15 上	16 戏
17 玩	18 电	19 脑	20 游

WRITING 3 Fill in the gaps with the correct characters according to the English.

1 小丽喜欢 __a__ (reading)，不喜欢 __b__ (watch TV)。

2 大明和弟弟会 __a__ (play ball games)。

3 英英星期六 __a__ (watch films)，星期日 __b__ (surf the Internet)。

94 九十四

3 读和写 dú hé xiě Reading and Writing B

❀ Extra reading and writing practice

READING 1 Translate the sentences into English.

1 我叫小欢，我会打乒乓球，不会踢足球。
2 我是小月，我喜欢上网，不喜欢玩儿滑板。
3 我叫天天，我星期六游泳，星期日买东西。
4 我是小星，我的爱好是跑步和玩儿电脑游戏。
5 我叫家家，我喜欢看电影和看电视，不喜欢打篮球。

READING 2 Read the passage below about Longlong and decide if the statements are true or false.

龙龙和他的家人有很多爱好。妈妈喜欢买东西和跑步；爸爸喜欢上网、打篮球和打网球。哥哥喜欢踢足球、玩儿滑板和玩儿电脑游戏。妹妹喜欢看电视。龙龙星期一和妈妈跑步，星期二和爸爸打篮球，星期六和哥哥玩儿电脑游戏，星期日和妹妹看电视。龙龙有一只狗，妹妹有一只猫。龙龙的狗喜欢看电视，妹妹的猫喜欢玩儿球。

1 Longlong's mum likes shopping and surfing the Internet.
2 His dad likes basketball and tennis.
3 His brother likes football and skateboard.
4 His sister likes computer games.
5 Longlong runs with his mum on Mondays.
6 He can play basketball.
7 He plays computer games with his dad.
8 He doesn't watch TV.
9 He has a dog and his sister has a cat.
10 The dog likes playing with balls and the cat likes watching TV.

WRITING 3 Write your diary according to the days and the pictures.

Monday Tuesday Wednesday Thursday Friday Saturday Sunday

九十五 95

4 读和写 dú hé xiě Reading and Writing A

❀ Extra reading and writing practice

READING 1 Match the school subjects with the pictures.

Example: **1 c**

| a 中文 | b 数学 | c 音乐 | d 地理 | e 德文 |
| f 体育 | g 英文 | h 法文 | i 科学 | j 历史 |

READING 2 Put the words in the correct order to form sentences.

1 a 四点二十分 / b 他 / c 下午 / d 放学 。

2 a 几点 / b 中文 / c 有 / d 星期四 / e 课 / f 你 ？

3 a 上午 / b 星期六 / c 打乒乓球 / d 我 / e 十点半 。

WRITING 3 Fill in the gaps according to the English.

__1__ (She is called) 小玉，今年 __2__ (sixteen years old)。她是 __3__ (Chinese)，她在 __4__ (Britain) 学英文。小玉的班不大，有七个 __5__ (female students)，九个 __6__ (male students)。他们 __7__ (in the morning) 学英文，__8__ (in the afternoon) 看电视、上网、__9__ (play ball games)。小玉上午八点 __10__ (go to school)，下午三点 __11__ (finish school)。她很 __12__ (like) 她的学校。

96 九十六

4 读和写 dú hé xiě Reading and Writing B

❈ Extra reading and writing practice

READING 1 Read the conversation between 玛丽 (Mary) and 大卫 (David) and answer the questions in English.

玛丽：早上好！

大卫：玛丽，早上好！

玛丽：你这个星期忙吗？

大卫：我这个星期很忙，你呢？

玛丽：我也很忙。我有很多课。

大卫：你有多少课？

玛丽：二十五节课。我有四节中文课、五节数学课、三节德文课，也有历史课、体育课……你呢？

大卫：我有二十三节课。我有数学课、中文课、音乐课和科学课，没有德文课和历史课。

玛丽：我不喜欢历史课。你喜欢吗？

大卫：我很喜欢。我星期六和星期日看历史书。你喜欢体育课吗？

玛丽：喜欢。我星期一下午两点二十分和星期三上午十一点有体育课。你几点放学？

大卫：下午三点半。你会玩儿滑板吗？

玛丽：会。星期五下午四点，我们玩儿滑板吧？

大卫：好！

1. How do David and Mary greet each other?
2. Why is Mary very busy this week?
3. How many maths lessons does Mary have this week?
4. How many lessons does David have this week?
5. What lessons doesn't David have?
6. What lesson doesn't Mary like and what lesson does she like?
7. On which days does David read history books?
8. When does Mary have PE lessons?
9. What time does David finish school?
10. What activity are they going to do on Friday afternoon?

WRITING 2 Use the characters below to make four sentences and translate them into English.

我 午 中 男 你 是 国 学 女 文 人 英 生 上

5 读和写 dú hé xiě Reading and Writing A

❀ Extra reading and writing practice

READING 1 Pick the odd one out and state the reason.

Example: **1 d** is the odd one out as it means 'water' which is the only drink.

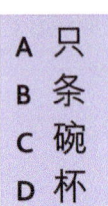

1 a 面包   b 面条   c 米饭   d 水
2 a 水   b 牛肉   c 茶   d 果汁
3 a 鸡蛋   b 米饭   c 包子   d 茶
4 a 炒面   b 水   c 吃   d 茶

READING 2 Choose the correct measure word to complete the phrase and then match the phrase with the correct picture.

Example: **1 C v**

一 _1_ 米饭
两 _2_ 果汁
四 _3_ 鸡蛋
一 _4_ 鱼
一 _5_ 鸡

A 只
B 条
C 碗
D 杯
E 个

WRITING 3 Complete the sentences according to the pictures.

Example: 1 水果

我早饭吃 _1_ 。

我午饭吃 _2_ 。

我晚饭吃 _3_ 和 _4_ 。

我 _5_ 吃 _6_ 、喝 _7_ 。

我早饭 _8_ 包子、_9_ 牛奶。

98 九十八

5 读和写 dú hé xiě Reading and Writing B

❀ Extra reading and writing practice

READING 1 The following people want to create their own English webpages. You need to help them put the information into English.

我叫…	生日	爱好	喜欢吃…	不喜欢吃…	宠物
文文	四月七日	上网	面包	水果	一只狗
小月	十月六日	打网球、打乒乓球	面条	炒面	三条鱼
大中	十二月三十日	看书	鸡肉	米饭	两只鸟
小欢	五月十八日	看电视	水果	饺子	一只鸡

My name	Birthday	Hobbies	Food liked	Food disliked	Pet
Wenwen					

READING 2 Read Liu Shu and Elaine's notes talking about what food they and their family members like/dislike.

刘数 Liú Shù: 我喜欢吃饺子、面条,我不喜欢吃米饭。我喜欢喝咖啡。我爸爸喜欢吃米饭,喜欢喝茶,不喜欢喝咖啡。我妈妈喜欢吃肉,她喜欢吃猪肉、牛肉、羊肉,也喜欢吃鸡肉。

Elaine: 我喜欢吃面包,喜欢喝水。我妈妈喜欢吃鸡肉炒面,喜欢喝中国茶。我爸爸不喜欢吃肉,他喜欢吃菜,他喜欢喝英国茶。

Who… 1 a likes coffee, and b dislikes it?
2 a likes eating rice, and b dislikes it?
3 a likes eating meat, and b dislikes meat?
4 likes fried noodles?
5 likes Chinese tea?

WRITING 3 You are replying to your Chinese friend's e-mail about going out to a restaurant. Tell your friend what your favourite food/drink is, and what you don't like to eat and drink.

"天一"饭馆很好,有米饭、面条、肉、菜。我喜欢吃"天一"饭馆的牛肉、炒面和饺子,我也想吃鸡肉炒面。你喜欢吃什么?

文天

三月十六日

九十九 99

语法 Grammar

Introduction

Chinese grammar is quite straightforward. This section of the book is here to help you, especially with revision, and you won't need to look through the whole book to find explanations. All the grammar in this book is covered. Each grammar point is accompanied by a clear description of how it works and when to use it, why it is important and what to watch out for. Where a grammar point is slightly more tricky, it is followed by exercises for you to practise the new grammar.

The explanations are split into the following topics:

- **Nouns**
    1 singular/plural nouns
    2 measure words for nouns
    3 pronouns and showing possession
- **Verbs**
    1 Chinese verbs don't change
    2 verb-objects
    3 liking (喜欢), wanting (想) and knowing how to (会)
    4 negatives
- **Adjectives**
- **Numbers**
- **Age**
- **Time and dates**
- **Word order**
    1 time words
    2 prepositions of place
- **Conjunctions (linking words)**
- **Asking questions**

名词 Nouns

1 Chinese: singular or plural?

How does it work and when do I use it?

Chinese nouns don't change in the plural. 看电影 can mean either 'watch films' (in general) or 'watch a film' (one film in particular). And if you say 我有哥哥 (literally 'I have big brothers'), you might mean one big brother, two big brothers or twenty big brothers. The noun (哥哥) will always stay the same, and the only way anybody else will know how many you mean is if you put a number in front of 哥哥:

我有二十个哥哥。 = I have twenty big brothers.

Why is it important?

Not having to learn lots of different plurals makes life easier; you just have to learn the character for a noun and that's it!

Things to watch out for

As Chinese nouns don't change between the singular and plural, it can be easy to make assumptions about a noun when you're reading. Beware of doing this – you need to look for evidence as to whether a noun is singular or plural. Is there a measure word? Is the number referred to later on in the passage? Look for clues.

2 Measure words for nouns

How does it work and when do I use it?

We also use measure words in English when describing a number of objects: one **cup** of tea or three **pieces** of paper. In Chinese, you always need to put a measure word between a number and the noun: *number + measure word + noun*. 个 ge is the most commonly used measure word. For example:

一个姐姐 yí ge jiě jie one older sister

三个弟弟 sān ge dì di three younger brothers

Different types of noun have different measure words. Here is a list of the ones you have learnt so far.

Measure word	Nouns
个 ge	the most frequently used measure word, people and places: 人、哥哥、妈妈、老师、学生、班、etc.
口 kǒu	members in a family: 我家有四口人
岁 suì	years of age: 我十二岁
只 zhī	some animals: 狗、猫、鸟、etc.
条 tiáo	long, winding, flexible things: 鱼、蛇
碗 wǎn	a bowl of: 面条、米饭、etc.
杯 bēi	a cup/glass of: 茶、咖啡、果汁、etc.

Why is it important?

Chinese grammar is very straightforward and often quite flexible. However, there are a few key things that you must do, and putting in a measure word between a number and a noun is one of them. Your Chinese won't sound right without it. If you can't remember which measure word you need, then just use 个; it is much better to do this than not use a measure word at all.

Things to watch out for

Don't forget that 二 èr changes to 两 liǎng before a measure word, so :

'two birds ' becomes 两只鸟 and

'two little sisters' becomes 两个妹妹

岁 suì acts as a measure word in its own right, so it doesn't need anything between it and the number : 我十一岁。

Try it out

Now is the chance for you to get some practice. Put the letter corresponding to the correct measure word into the numbered gaps in the passage below.

我叫 Maddy。我十四 _1_ 。
我家有八 _2_ 人：爸爸、妈妈、三 _3_ 弟弟、
两 _4_ 妹妹和我。我也有一 _5_ 蛇和五 _6_ 猫。
我晚上吃三 _7_ 米饭，喝四 _8_ 果汁。

a	个	e	岁
b	只	f	口
c	杯	g	条
d	个	h	碗

3 Pronouns and showing possession

How does it work and when do I use it?

Chinese pronouns are very easy, as you only have to learn three and then add 们 on the end to make them plural. This is much easier than having to learn that the plural of 'I' is 'we'.

我	I	我们	we
你	you	你们	you (plural)
他/她	he/she	他们/她们	they

To make 'I' into 'my' is very simple too. You just add 的 and then follow it with the appropriate noun, for example: 我的生日 = my birthday.

我	I	我的	my
你	you	你的	your
他/她	he/she	他的/她的	his/her
我们	we	我们的	our
你们	you (plural)	你们的	your (plural)
他们/她们	they	他们的/她们的	their

For example:

我们的爱好是打网球。= Our hobby is playing tennis.

Grammar

Why is it important?

的 is important in Chinese and will crop up again and again in different ways. As its use becomes more complicated, it can cause confusion, so it is important to try to understand each different usage as you meet it. Then it won't cause you any problems.

Things to watch out for

的 is often omitted where the relationship between the nouns and possessive is close, for example 我爸爸 = my father, 我姐姐 = my older sister, 我们班 = our class. When reading, look at the sentence carefully so as not to muddle 'I/my', 'he/his', etc. If there is a 的 after 我 and 他, then it is 'my' and 'his'. However, if there is a verb (but no 的) after 我 and 他, then it means 'I' and 'he'. Beware of jumping to conclusions.

Try it out

Now is the chance for you to get some practice. Read the passage and note down the numbers of the gaps that need 的. Not all of the gaps will need it.

我 __1__ 家有五口人。我 __2__ 姐姐是学生。她会说中文。
她 __3__ 班有四十个学生。他们 __4__ 喜欢学中文，也喜欢学法文。
我们 __5__ 星期四下午三点有中文课。他们 __6__ 中文老师很好。

动词 Verbs

1 Chinese verbs don't change

How does it work and when do I use it?

A Chinese verb always stays the same. Let's look at 有 yǒu 'to have' and 吃 chī 'to eat' as examples.

'I have' = 我有; 'you have' = 你有; 'he/she has' = 他/她有;
'we have' = 我们有; 'you (plural) have' = 你们有; 'they have' = 他们有
'we eat' = 我们吃; 'they eat' = 他们吃

Why is it important?

When you are struggling with learning characters, it is important to remember the advantages of learning Chinese. Think how long it takes to learn verb endings in other languages.

Things to watch out for

As you learn more Chinese, you will find that time words ('yesterday', 'tomorrow', 'next year', etc.) show the time frame of a Chinese sentence, sometimes accompanied by suffixes which go after the verb. Remember that the verb itself never changes, but watch out as you progress with the language for clues about the time frame of the sentence or passage.

Try it out

Now is the chance for you to get some practice. Try translating the following sentences into English.

1 她是我妈妈。
2 他们是我的老师。
3 我们今天下午有英文课。
4 他们今天晚上看电视。
5 我不想喝茶。

2 Verb-objects

How does it work and when do I use it?

Many Chinese verbs take an object, such as : 看书 kàn shū = 'to read books' (or 'reading'), 吃饭 chī fàn = 'to eat food/rice' (or 'eating'), 踢足球 tī zú qiú = 'to play football', 看电影 kàn diàn yǐng = 'to watch films' (or 'a film').

Why is it important?

If you miss out the object of a verb-object construction, it feels like something is missing, and what you are trying to say may not make sense. In English we can say 'I like reading' or 'I like eating', but in Chinese 我喜欢看 or 我喜欢吃 will make the listener ask 'What? What is it that you like reading or eating?' At the very least, you need to say 我喜欢吃饭。 ('I like eating' – the 'food' is understood), but you may want to say something more specific, for instance 我喜欢吃面条。 'I like eating noodles.'

Things to watch out for

You need to remember that if you do say something specific, such as 'I like eating dumplings', you say 我喜欢吃饺子。 (You name the specific food after 吃.) You do not need two objects:

我喜欢吃饺子饭。 This sentence is wrong; it literally means 'I like eating dumpling-food.'

Try it out

Pick the right object from the box to match the verbs in the paragraph below describing Xiao Li's day. Write down the correct letter to fill the gap.

a 东西   b 网   c 书   d 乒乓球   e 早饭   f 步   g 中文

小李八点吃 _1_ ，九点上 _2_ 。
她十一点打 _3_ ，十二点看 _4_ 。
她下午两点学 _5_ ，四点买 _6_ 。

3 Liking, wanting and knowing how (喜欢、想、会)

How does it work and when do I use it?
These are often called auxiliary verbs: 'I like running', 'I would like to eat Beijing roast duck', 'They can speak Chinese'. In European languages, which all have verb changes, these auxiliary verbs can be tricky to use, but in Chinese it is much simpler.

Why is it important?
You need to be able to use these verbs to express yourself in Chinese with some variation rather than just saying: 'I eat, I run, I study, I sleep'.

Things to watch out for
All you need to do is to learn these words. The only thing to watch out for is the difference between 喜欢 xǐ huan ('to like') and 想 xiǎng ('want/would like'). Because the initial sound in pinyin (xi) is very similar, there can sometimes be confusion.

我喜欢看电视。= I like watching TV.

我想看电视。= I want to/would like to watch TV.

Try it out
Have a quick revision session with these auxiliary verbs by translating the following into English.

1 我们会游泳。
2 他想喝果汁。
3 他们喜欢跑步。
4 她会踢足球。
5 你喜欢玩儿电脑游戏吗？

4 Negatives

How does it work and when do I use it?

The negative of most verbs is made by adding 不 in front of the verb. For example:

我不上网。 = I don't surf the Internet.

他不看电影。 = He doesn't watch films.

However, the verb 有 yǒu ('to have') is different. It is made into a negative by putting 没 méi in front of it:

我没有狗。 = I don't have a dog/dogs.

Why is it important?

There is no single word for 'yes' or 'no' in Chinese – if someone asks you a yes/no question, usually you repeat the verb in the question to say 'yes', and make the verb negative to say 'no'. So it is important that you know how to make a negative.

Things to watch out for

Where there is an auxiliary verb plus a verb in a sentence, you need to make sure you put the negative in front of the verb you are negating:

我不喜欢玩儿滑板。 = I don't like skateboarding.

Verbs are quite easy in Chinese without tenses, but using 不 with 有 is wrong. Try to avoid it.

Try it out

Use either **a** 不 or **b** 没 to complete the following sentences and translate into English.

我 _1_ 是老师。

他们 _2_ 想吃牛肉。

她 _3_ 有弟弟、妹妹。

今天你 _4_ 有数学课。

我们 _5_ 会打乒乓球。

Grammar

形容词 Adjectives

How does it work and when do I use it?

For a simple one-syllable or one-character adjective (describing word), such as 大 dà ('big') or 小 xiǎo ('small'), you just need to add it before the noun you're describing:

一只大猫 = one big cat

三只小狗 = three small dogs

Don't forget that you still need the correct measure word.

数字 Numbers

How does it work and when do I use it?

Learning numbers in Chinese is really easy! For numbers between 10 and 20 you just say '10 1', '10 2', and so on: 十一, 十二… For higher numbers, you say '2 10', '3 10', etc.: 二十, 三十, so 42 would be '4 10 2' or 四十二.

Why is it important?

It's important to give your numbers as much practice as possible. Numbers are crucial in everyday Chinese because the days of the week and months of the year use numbers instead of names. You will learn about Chinese money in the next book.

Things to watch out for

Don't forget that 二 èr changes to 两 liǎng before a measure word, so:

'two dogs' becomes 两只狗 and

'two cups of tea' becomes 两杯茶

Try it out

Now try revising your number writing. The following sentences have numbers instead of characters. In your exercise book write down the characters for the numbers given.

1. 我们班有 39 个学生。
2. 他想喝 7 杯水。
3. 爸爸有 3 个弟弟。
4. 你有 12 条鱼。
5. 我想吃 56 个鸡蛋。
6. 她的班有 64 个学生。

年龄 Age

How does it work and when do I use it?

In English, when you talk about someone's age, you say *person* + *verb 'to be'* (am/is/are) + *age*, 'I am 11 years old'. But in Chinese it's simple: you just need to say: *person* + *age* (*number* + 岁 suì): 我八岁。 wǒ bā suì ('I am eight years old').

Why is it important?

Chinese people often ask about age, even after you have reached adulthood, so it is good to be able to answer the question. Remember, if you want to find out someone else's age, then you need to be able to say 你多大？ nǐ duō dà ('How old are you?').

Things to watch out for

Don't forget to use 两 if you want to say 我妹妹两岁。 ('My little sister is two years old'). However, this is only for two, not 12, 22, etc.

时间和日期 Time and dates

How does it work and when do I use it?

Telling the time is quite straightforward if you remember that 点 diǎn = 'o'clock' and 分 fēn = 'minute'. You can then say '8.25' by saying 八点二十五分. If you want to say '8.30', then you can use 半 bàn ('half') and say 八点半.

Days of the week: The days of the week in Chinese are very simple as well. Starting with Monday, you just put the number of the day (one, two, etc.) after 星期 xīng qī ('week'): 星期二 for Tuesday; and so on. The only different one is Sunday, which doesn't use a number: it's 星期日 or 星期天. You use 天 tiān more often when you are talking, but you may see 日 rì more in a book or newspaper.

Months of the year: 月 yuè is the Chinese word for 'month'. You just need to add the right number before 月 to make a month: for example, 一月 for January, 二月 for February, etc.

Dates: the day of the month is just a number followed by 日, so 5 April becomes 四月五日. Don't forget that in Chinese you always say the month first and then the date.

Why is it important?

People talk a lot about times in real life. Also, times and dates are always tested in exams. They are not hard, and if you know how to express times and dates, it will give you confidence when listening in Chinese.

Things to watch out for

As with other uses of numbers, it is important to remember 两. If you want to say '2 o'clock', it is 两点. However, remember that 'Tuesday' is always 星期二 and that 'February' is always 二月.

The days of the week are easy, but 星期 is a difficult word to say. Practise saying it with a friend until you are both confident.

Remember that the day of the week comes after 星期 (星期三 'Wednesday'), but that the number of the month comes before 月: for example, 三月 is 'March'.

Try it out

Match the characters in the box with the English below.

a 十点半　　b 星期五　　c 一月五日　　d 六点五十分
e 星期日　　f 两点十分　g 十月三十一日　h 星期二

1　Sunday　　　　5　Friday
2　5 January　　　6　ten to seven
3　ten past two　　7　31 October
4　half past ten　　8　Tuesday

词序 Word order

1 Time words

How does it work and when do I use it?

The order of time words in a Chinese sentence is always from the general (the month, the day of the week, etc.) to the most specific (the time). For example:

我星期一上午十点有体育课。 (literally: 'I Monday morning 10am have PE.')

我星期日下午四点半打篮球。 (literally: 'I Sunday afternoon 4.30pm play basketball.')

Time words come before the verb, which means they are at the very beginning of a sentence or straight after the subject.

When you say what you have for breakfast, lunch, etc., you put the words in the following order:

subject (I, he, she, mum etc.) + *meal* (breakfast, etc.) + *verb phrase*.

我+午饭+吃炒面。 = I + lunch + eat fried noodles. = I have fried noodles for lunch.

The time word (lunch) comes early in the sentence.

Why is it important?

Chinese grammar can often be quite flexible, but some things are definitely wrong, and not putting time words in the right order is one of them.

Things to watch out for

In English you usually put the time at the end of the sentence. For example, in English you say 'I'm not surfing the Internet this morning'. In Chinese you say

今天早上我不上网。 or 我今天早上不上网。

Try it out

First translate the sentences into English and then write the dates in Chinese characters.

1　我星期一下午四点半打篮球。　　4　Wednesday 14 March
2　哥哥星期天学中文。　　　　　　5　Friday 29 November
3　我们下午五点十分吃饭。　　　　6　Saturday 22 November

2 Prepositions of place

How does it work and when do I use it?

在 is a preposition of place and means 'in', 'on' or 'at'. The sentence structure for 在 is: *subject* + 在 + *place* + *verb*. For example:

姐姐在北京学习。 jiě jie zài běi jīng xué xí = My older sister is studying in Beijing. (literally 'My older sister in Beijing is studying.')

我在家上网。 wǒ zài jiā shàng wǎng = I surf the Internet at home.

Why is it important?

Chinese grammar can be quite flexible, but some things are definitely wrong, and getting place words out of order is one of them.

Things to watch out for

It is really easy to get this word order wrong and put it in the English word order. Try not to do this.

连词 Conjunctions (linking words)

How does it work and when do I use it?

There are several different ways of saying 'and' in Chinese. One of them is 和 hé, which is only used between nouns. It is not used to connect clauses or sentences in Chinese. Notice the difference:

爸爸和妈妈 = Dad and Mum; but

爸爸叫 Robert, 妈妈叫 Selina. = Dad is called Robert, (and) Mum is called Selina.

也 yě means 'also' or 'too'. Its position is always just after the subject and before the verb in Chinese sentences. For example, 'I like swimming, too' in Chinese is 我也喜欢游泳。 The 也 is placed between 我 and 喜欢.

Why is it important?

There are not too many hard and fast Chinese grammar rules, but getting 也 in the wrong place or using 和 to connect whole sentences are really mistakes you should take particular care to avoid.

Things to watch out for

Remember that 也 means 'too', especially when you are translating. If you were asked to say 'I like playing football too' in Chinese, don't spend time worrying about how to translate 'too'; it is just the same word as 'also', so the translation would be 我也喜欢踢足球。

Grammar

问问题 Asking questions

How does it work and when do I use it?
Below is a quick revision of the types of question you have had in this book.

你多大？

To ask someone's age, you don't even need to use a verb, you just use the question word and the pronoun or name ('you', 'he', 'she', 'Jade', etc.).

So in English we say 'How old are you?' This becomes 你多大？ nǐ duō dà (literally: 'You how big?').

你叫什么？

When asking names, the question word goes at the end of the sentence.

What is your name? = 你叫什么？ nǐ jiào shén me (literally: 'You are called what?')

Using 吗

When you ask a yes/no question (questions that normally need a yes or no when you answer them in English), you just need to add 吗 ma at the end of the sentence to turn it into a yes/no question.

Statement	Yes/no question
你有狗。	你有狗吗？
Jennifer 有弟弟。	Jennifer 有弟弟吗？

To answer the questions, repeat the verb to say 'yes' (有) and make it into a negative to say 'no' (没有).

Using 谁 shéi, 'Who?'

谁 can be used at the beginning or end of a question, wherever the answer to 'Who?' is required. When you use question words like this in Chinese, you don't have to change the order as you do in English. Then you answer by taking out the question word and replacing it with the answer. For example:

他是谁？ = Who is he? (literally: 'He is who?')
他是我哥哥。 = He is my elder brother.
谁喜欢看书？ = Who likes reading?
小明喜欢看书。 = Xiaoming likes reading.

Using 几 jǐ, ('how many', 'how much')

几 is a question word for asking 'how much' when you expect a low number (10 or less) in reply. It is always used with a measure word. Its place in a question depends on where the answer is going to be. For example:

今天星期几？ jīn tiān xīng qī jǐ = What day of the week is it today?
今天星期五。 jīn tiān xīng qī wǔ = Today is Friday.
几点？ jǐ diǎn = What time is it?
七点。 qī diǎn = It is seven o'clock

一百十一 **111**

多少 duō shǎo 'How many? How much?'

多少 also means 'how many' or 'how much'. However, 多少 is used for a number more than 10 and you can use it without a measure word. For example:

你们班有多少学生？ nǐ men bān yǒu duō shǎo xué sheng = How many students are there in your class?

多少人会踢足球？ duō shǎo rén huì tī zú qiú = How many people can play football?

Why is it important?

Forgetting how to ask a question when learning a foreign language is very common. In class, it is more often you who are answering the questions rather than asking them. You need to be able to take the lead in a conversation too.

Things to watch out for

The important thing is that where question words are used, you just take out the question word and put in the answer – no worrying about word order in this case.

For example, 你是谁？ = You are who?

我是小李。 = I am Little Li.

写汉字 Writing Chinese characters

You have learnt quite a lot about the evolution of Chinese characters and how to write them in the course of this book and will continue to build up this knowledge when you move on to Jìn bù 2. This section is to help you revise writing characters and develop your own ways of memorising them. Learning characters is quite hard work, but also fun and rewarding.

Strokes in a Chinese character

The basic strokes in a Chinese character are listed below with their names in English and Chinese.

	Stroke	Chinese	English	Examples
1	丶	点 diǎn	the dot	小 六
2	一	横 héng	the horizontal stroke, written left to right	一 有
3	丨	竖 shù	the vertical stroke, written top to bottom	十 中
4	丿	撇 piě	the sweeping left stroke, written top right to bottom left	人 爱
5	乀	捺 nà	the sweeping right stroke, written top left to bottom right	八 欢
6	㇀	提 tí	the rising stroke, written from bottom left to top right	汉 习
7	亅	钩 gōu	the hook, can be written in any direction	到 对

Tip
Some people like to learn the names of the strokes and say them as they draw each character – in English or Chinese. Try it and see if it helps you.

Stroke order for writing Chinese characters

Here are the basic rules for stroke order for writing a Chinese character using characters you've learnt in this book as examples.

1. Write from left to right.   北 川
2. Write from top to bottom.   三 下
3. Write horizontals before verticals.   十 羊
4. Write left falling before right falling.   人 入
5. Write from outside frame to inside strokes.   月 同
6. Write major middle stroke before the two sides.   小 水
7. Finish what is inside the box before you close it.   日 四

一百十三 113

叫	丨	口	口	叨	叫
三	一	二	三		
十	一	十			
八	丿	八			
月	丿	几	月	月	
小	亅	小	小		
四	丨	冂	四	四	四

Try it out

Make sure you remember these rules by having a go at writing the characters below using the correct stroke order and building them up stroke by stroke. Copy and complete the grid. Ask your teacher to check your work.

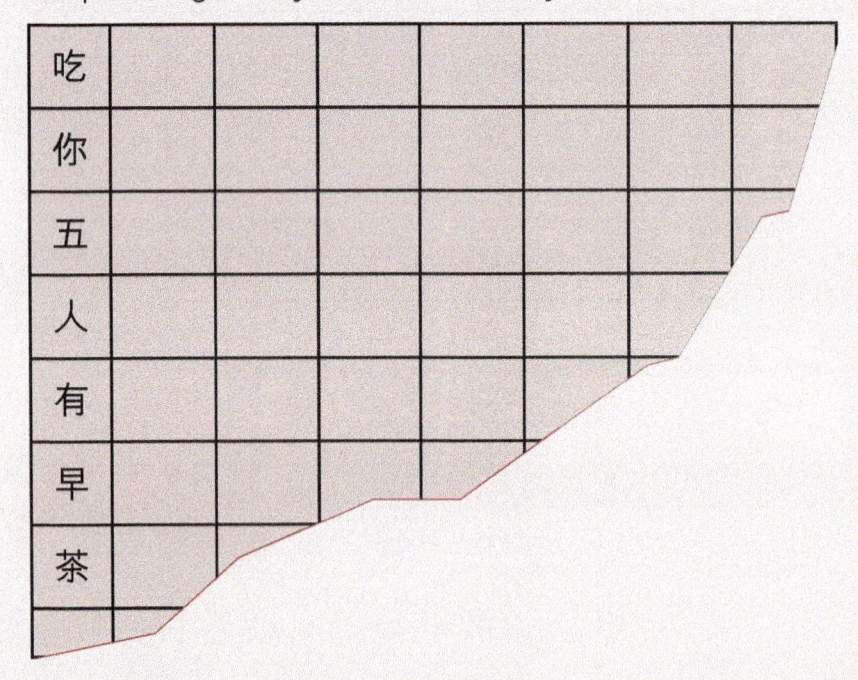

吃								
你								
五							
人						
有					
早				
茶			

Tip

You may wonder why stroke order is necessary if you are not writing your characters with a brush and ink. Having a methodical approach and always writing frequently recurring elements in characters with the same stroke order will help you remember them; it is very hard otherwise. Also, as you progress, you will need to know exactly how many strokes there are in a character in order to be able to use a Chinese dictionary; that means your stroke writing must be accurate.

Writing Chinese characters

Radicals

As you know, radicals may give you a clue to the meaning of a character. The table below gives you the meaning of some common radicals.

口	mouth	吃
女	female	妈
犭	animal	猫
目	eye	看
扌	hand	打
氵	(three drops of) water	汁
讠	speech	说
囗	an enclosed area	国
饣	meal	饭
火	fire	炒
艹	grass/plant	茶
石	stone	碗
舌	tongue	甜
车	vehicle (with wheels)	辆
日	sun, day	晴
忄	(vertical) heart	忙
亻	person	你
力	strength	男
土	earth	场
子	child	孩
辶	running	过
木	wood	树

Tip
Some learners like to work out the radical for some of the characters they learn and relate it to its meaning; this helps them memorise the character.

一百十五 115

Ten ideas for learning Chinese characters

1. Practise your Chinese characters regularly a few at a time. It can be quite a relaxing break from other school work. Don't try to learn too many in one go.
2. Develop your own method for remembering them. While some students chant strokes or learn radicals, others find it helpful to look for pictures in the characters; linking an imaginary picture with the real meaning can help in jogging the memory. Look for patterns or repeated components in groups you are learning.
3. Make sure you are methodical. There will be some which you find easy. These don't need to be practised every day, but you still need to revisit them quite often. There will be some – there always are – that you find particularly hard. Make sure you give them extra attention.
4. Develop a learning schedule with either flashcards or a computer programme.
5. Look at online Chinese learning programmes (there are many on the Internet) and computer games in order to improve your character recognition, which will make it easier to learn to write.
6. Stick post-it notes all over your house with Chinese characters on, so that you see the ones you are learning frequently.
7. Remember that calligraphy is an art form. Have a go at writing characters with a brush and ink.
8. Don't get frustrated; it gets easier with time.
9. Have a look at books/websites on the origin of characters.
10. Be positive and enjoy it!

Writing Chinese characters

Pinyin

Pinyin is the romanisation of Chinese characters with the appropriate tone markers. Pinyin is not a language in its own right; it is just a pronunciation guide to the sounds of Mandarin Chinese. The characters give you very few clues about how to pronounce them. Pinyin was developed first to standardise pronunciation in Chinese schools, where everybody learns Mandarin Chinese, even if they speak another dialect in the playground or at home. Have a look on the Internet about the dialects of the Chinese language if you are interested.

Most Chinese people then forget pinyin after primary school and only use it occasionally when inputting characters on a computer. You too must focus on characters and remember that pinyin often does not sound how it looks; you will already have found this out during the course of this book.

Tones

To pronounce Chinese properly, you need to understand tones. Many characters have the same sound in Chinese; using the correct tones will help make sure that the person listening knows what you are talking about. However, most listeners get a lot from the context of what you are saying too, so you don't need to worry **too** much about tones; it is best just to relax and imitate rather than worry in advance about the tones for a sentence/phrase you want to say. There are four main tones in Mandarin:

- **1st tone**: high and flat: sān 三
- **2nd tone**: going up: shí 十
- **3rd tone**: down and up: wǔ 五
- **4th tone**: going down: liù 六

Tones always stay the same for a character, except in two instances. Don't be concerned about these; you just need to be aware of them. If you use your ears well, the right tone at the right time will come naturally over time.

不 bù not – this character is a fourth tone, but its pronunciation changes to a second tone if the character which follows it is a fourth tone, for example 我不上网。wǒ bú shàng wǎng = I don't surf the Internet.

一 yī one – this character is a first tone. However, its pronunciation changes to a second tone if it is before a fourth tone, for example 我有一个 yí ge 姐姐 (even though ge is not given a tone in pinyin, it is in fact a fourth tone). If 一 yī is followed by a second or third tone then it changes into a fourth tone itself, for example 一条 yì tiáo 鱼.

辞典 Glossary

a	a cat	一只猫	yì zhī māo
	a bowl of rice	一碗米饭	yì wǎn mǐ fàn
	a younger brother	一个弟弟	yí ge dì di
age	I am 8 years old.	我八岁。	wǒ bā suì
	How old are you?	你多大?	nǐ duō dà
also	I like history, (I) also like geography.	我喜欢历史, (我)也喜欢地理。	wǒ xǐ huan lì shǐ (wǒ) yě xǐ huan dì lǐ
and	I like basketball and tennis.	我喜欢篮球和网球。	wǒ xǐ huan lán qiú hé wǎng qiú
	My younger sister is called Wenwen and she is five years old.	我妹妹叫文文, 她五岁。	wǒ mèi mei jiào wén wen tā wǔ suì
at/in	He plays football in school.	他在学校踢足球。	tā zài xué xiào tī zú qiú
to be	My name is…	我叫…	wǒ jiào…
	Today is Tuesday.	今天是星期二。	jīn tiān shì xīng qī èr
	I am 11 years old.	我十一岁。	wǒ shí yī suì
birthday	Today is my birthday.	今天是我的生日。	jīn tiān shì wǒ de shēng rì
busy	I am very busy.	我很忙。	wǒ hěn máng
	Are you busy?	你忙不忙?	nǐ máng bu máng
to buy	to buy things (go shopping)	买东西	mǎi dōng xi
can (know how to)	I can swim.	我会游泳。	wǒ huì yóu yǒng
	I can't play tennis.	我不会打网球。	wǒ bú huì dǎ wǎng qiú
country/ nationality	China/Chinese	中国/中国人	zhōng guó/zhōng guó rén
	Britain/British	英国/英国人	yīng guó/yīng guó rén
dates/ months	6 March	三月六日	sān yuè liù rì
	My birthday is 14 January.	我的生日是一月十四日。	wǒ de shēng rì shì yī yuè shí sì rì
Days of the week	Monday	星期一	xīng qī yī
	Tuesday	星期二	xīng qī èr
	Wednesday	星期三	xīng qī sān
	Thursday	星期四	xīng qī sì
	Friday	星期五	xīng qī wǔ
	Saturday	星期六	xīng qī liù
	Sunday	星期日	xīng qī rì

Glossary – English/Chinese

to drink	I drink fruit juice.	我喝果汁。	wǒ hē guǒ zhī
drinks	water	水	shuǐ
	tea	茶	chá
	milk	牛奶	niú nǎi
	coffee	咖啡	kā fēi
	juice	果汁	guǒ zhī
to eat	(My) younger brother doesn't eat breakfast.	弟弟不吃早饭。	dì di bù chī zǎo fàn
family	My family has three people.	我家有三口人。	wǒ jiā yǒu sān kǒu rén
	Xiaoyue's family is in China.	小月家在中国。	xiǎo yuè jiā zài zhōng guó
family members	dad	爸爸	bà ba
	mum	妈妈	mā ma
	older brother	哥哥	gē ge
	older sister	姐姐	jiě jie
	younger brother	弟弟	dì di
	younger sister	妹妹	mèi mei
food (savoury)	bread	面包	miàn bāo
	rice	米饭	mǐ fàn
	noodles	面条	miàn tiáo
	fried rice	炒饭	chǎo fàn
	fried noodles	炒面	chǎo miàn
	dumplings	饺子	jiǎo zi
	steamed stuffed bun	包子	bāo zi
good	Good morning.	早上好。	zǎo shang hǎo
	Goodbye.	再见。	zài jiàn
to have	She has a dog.	她有一只狗。	tā yǒu yì zhī gǒu
	I do not have an older brother.	我没有哥哥。	wǒ méi yǒu gē ge
hello	Hello.	你好。	nǐ hǎo
	Hello teacher.	老师好。	lǎo shī hǎo
I/you/he/she	I am called (My name is) Edmund.	我叫 Edmund。	wǒ jiào Edmund
	She is Safina.	她是 Safina。	tā shì Safina
	You would like (to drink) tea, and he would like (to drink) coffee.	你想喝茶,他想喝咖啡。	nǐ xiǎng hē chá tā xiǎng hē kā fēi

一百十九 119

languages	Chinese	中文	zhōng wén
	English	英文	yīng wén
	German	德文	dé wén
	French	法文	fǎ wén
to like/ dislike	I like going online.	我喜欢上网。	wǒ xǐ huan shàng wǎng
	He doesn't like eating chicken.	他不喜欢吃鸡肉。	tā bù xǐ huan chī jī ròu
to listen	to listen to music	听音乐	tīng yīn yuè
male/female	male students	男(学)生	nán (xué) sheng
	female students	女(学)生	nǚ (xué) sheng
meal	breakfast	早饭	zǎo fàn
	lunch	午饭	wǔ fàn
	supper	晚饭	wǎn fàn
	Dad eats eggs for breakfast.	爸爸早饭吃鸡蛋。	bà ba zǎo fàn chī jī dàn
measure words	five people (total of a family)	五口人	wǔ kǒu rén
	one older sister	一个姐姐	yí ge jiě jie
	two cats	两只猫	liǎng zhī māo
	three fish	三条鱼	sān tiáo yú
	one bowl of noodles	一碗面条	yì wǎn miàn tiáo
	four glasses/cups of water	四杯水	sì bēi shuǐ
meat	pork	猪肉	zhū ròu
	beef	牛肉	niú ròu
	lamb/mutton	羊肉	yáng ròu
	chicken	鸡肉	jī ròu
name	My name is (I am called) Dazhong.	我叫大中。	wǒ jiào dà zhōng
	He is called William.	他叫 William。	tā jiào William
no/not	not good/small	不好/小	bù hǎo/xiǎo
	I do not eat pork.	我不吃猪肉。	wǒ bù chī zhū ròu
	They are not students.	他们不是学生。	tā men bú shì xué sheng
pets	one cat	一只猫	yì zhī māo
	one dog	一只狗	yì zhī gǒu
	three snakes	三条蛇	sān tiáo shé
	two fish	两条鱼	liǎng tiáo yú
	four birds	四只鸟	sì zhī niǎo
	one rabbit	一只兔子	yì zhī tù zi

to play	to play on the computer	玩儿电脑	wánr diàn nǎo
	to play on a skateboard	玩儿滑板	wánr huá bǎn
	to play basketball/ping pong/tennis	打篮球/乒乓球/网球	dǎ lán qiú/pīng pāng qiú/wǎng qiú
	to play football	踢足球	tī zú qiú
questions	Do you like watching films?	你喜欢看电影吗?	nǐ xǐ huan kàn diàn yǐng ma
	What is your name?	你叫什么?	nǐ jiào shén me
	What day is it today?	今天星期几?	jīn tiān xīng qī jǐ
	How many students do your class have?	你们班有多少学生?	nǐ men bān yǒu duō shǎo xué sheng
	Who is he?	他是谁?	tā shì shéi
	I want to watch TV, how about you?	我想看电视,你呢?	wǒ xiǎng kàn diàn shì nǐ ne
	What time do you have lunch?	你几点吃午饭?	nǐ jǐ diǎn chī wǔ fàn
to read/reading	Reading is my hobby.	看书是我的爱好。	kàn shū shì wǒ de ài hào
school	school	学校	xué xiào
	to go to school	上学	shàng xué
	to finish school	放学	fàng xué
	class	班	bān
	lesson	课	kè
school subjects	science	科学	kē xué
	maths	数学	shù xué
	history	历史	lì shǐ
	geography	地理	dì lǐ
	PE	体育	tǐ yù
	music	音乐	yīn yuè
sports	(to take part in) sports	运动	yùn dòng
	to run/running	跑步	pǎo bù
	to swim/swimming	游泳	yóu yǒng
	to play/playing ball games (except football)	打球	dǎ qiú
time/time of a day	a.m.	上午	shàng wǔ
	noon	中午	zhōng wǔ
	p.m.	下午	xià wǔ
	ten past three	三点十分	sān diǎn shí fēn
	I eat my breakfast at half past seven.	我七点半吃早饭。	wǒ qī diǎn bàn chī zǎo fàn

一百二十一 121

to want/ would like to	I would like to drink milk.	我想喝牛奶。	wǒ xiǎng hē niú nǎi
	He doesn't want to eat fried noodles.	他不想吃炒面。	tā bù xiǎng chī chǎo miàn
we/they/you (plural)	we	我们	wǒ men
	they	他/她们	tā/tā men
	you (plural)	你们	nǐ men
to watch	to watch (a) film	看电影	kàn diàn yǐng
	to watch TV	看电视	kàn diàn shì